Learning Resources Centre

To renew your loans:

108468

  Call us: 01227 811166

  Email:
LRC@canterburycollege.ac.uk

Text us: 07860023340
Text "RENEW", with your name
& Student ID number

Online:
tiny.cc/renew-my-books

Please see below for the date your book/item is due back.

Canterbury
College

L·R·C

Money and Teens: Savvy Money Skills
Copyright © 2012 Wes Karchut and Darby Karchut

Published by Copper Square Studios
Colorado Springs, CO
ISBN 978-0-9741145-3-8

Library of Congress Control Number: 2012919787

Karchut, Wesley, 1953—
    Money and teens: savvy money skills / by Wesley
    Karchut with Darby Karchut
    p. 192 22cm

ISBN 978-0-9741145-3-8 (pbk:alk. paper)—
ISBN 978-0-9741145-2-1(eBook)
Summary: A practical guide empowering teens to manage
their money for a better future.
1. Finance Personal—juvenile literature. 2. Children—
Finance Personal, juvenile literature. 3. Money—juvenile
literature. I. Karchut, Wesley, 1953—II. Karchut, Darby.
III. Title
HG179.C5359 2012
332.024—dc22
2012929787

This publication contains the opinions and ideas of the
authors. It is sold with the understanding that neither the
authors nor the publisher is engaged in rendering legal, tax,
investment, financial, accounting or other professional advice and services. The strategies contained in this book may
not be suitable for every individual and are not guaranteed

to produce or warranted to produce any particular results.

No warranty is made with respect to the accuracy or completeness of the information contained herein and both the authors and publishers specifically disclaim any responsibility for any liability, loss or risk, personal or otherwise, which is incurred as a consequence, directly or indirectly, of the use and application of any of the contents of this book.

iPhone®, iPad® and iTunes® are registered trademarks of Apple, Inc. Amazon.com® is a registered trademark of Amazon.com, Inc. Walmart® is a registered trademark of Walmart, Inc. eBay® is a registered tradeamrk of eBay, Inc. PayPal® is a registered trademark of PayPal, Inc.

All characters appearing in this work have been created solely for illustrative purposes. Any resemblance to real persons, living or dead, is purely coincidental.

Acknowledgements

The authors wish to acknowledge the following organizations, government resources and individuals for their invaluable assistance in the preparation of this book.

Fair Isaac and Company
Bank of America
Charles Schwab
Federal Deposit Insurance Coverage
Federal Housing Authority
Brankrate.com
Federal Reserve Board of Governors
United States Department of Education
United States Department of the Treasury
Federal Deposit Insurance Coverage
H&R Block
Federal Trade Commission
Sharon Honeycutt, Editor
Kaci Guthrie, M.Ed.

Contents

4 More About Debt

5 Credit Score Savvy

6 Money Psychology

7 Your Financial Statement

8 Budgeting Savvy

9 Checking Account Savvy

10 Electronic Banking

11   Tax Savvy

12   Compound Interest and Loans

13   Student Loan Savvy

Appendix A   More About Taxes

Index

Introduction

What are your dreams? An iPhone? A new computer? Spring break at the beach? According to a recent survey of teens, the most popular choices are the three C's—college, cars, and computers.

And, what does it take for these dreams to come true? Money. Although money is as hard to come by as ever, thousands of teens just like you have found all the money they need to live the life of their dreams. Are these teens rich? Are they smarter than you? Are they just lucky?

The answer is no, but what many of them do have is "money mojo." Mojo comes from African-American folklore and refers to an amulet or pouch containing magical charms. This book contains magical financial charms you can use right away to help you reach your dreams.

This book opens the doors to your future

The three C's could also be thought of in terms of financial goals:

Computers	=	Short-term goals
Cars	=	Medium-term goals
College	=	Long-term goals

These may be your goals as well, or you may have completely different ones. Which ones your choose doesn't matter. What does matter is that you set goals and then believe you can achieve them. However, believing by itself will not make money fall from of the sky or suddenly materialize in your wallet. You must also invest the time to read this book and apply what you have learned. But, if you make the effort, your dreams can happen.

Setting short, medium, and long-term goals gives you motivation to stay on track because the rewards will also be short, medium, and long-term. As you begin to see your efforts rewarded, you will discover the power of consistently applying what you have learned.

This book is a toolkit you can use not only now, but for the rest of your life. You wouldn't try to build a house without a hammer, saw, and level, nor make clothes without needles, thread, and scissors. Yet, how many teens, as well as adults, try to manage their money without an understanding of the basic tools of personal finance? According to the same teen survey mentioned above, only 60 percent of teens aged 16 to 18 know how to write a check; 40 percent don't know the difference between a debit card and a credit card; and only 35 percent know how to balance a checkbook.

Every day, the headlines are filled with stories about teens who have carelessly borrowed money. To pay it all back will take years; and for some, even this may not be enough time. In 2010, the average college graduate's student loan debt reached unprecedented levels, topping $25,000 — exceeding even credit cards and auto loans. If not properly managed, these debts will haunt these college graduates for years.

Your future can be different. But only if you understand the basics of personal finance.

Unlocking the secrets in this book

Studies have shown that over fifty percent of readers never bother to read more than the first chapter of a book. If this describes you, don't despair; you can still benefit from this text. Included at the end of this introduction is a short overview of the key concepts covered in each chapter, called *Money and Teens in a Nutshell*. If you review only these concepts, at a minimum you will gain a basic sense of what personal finance is all about. Of course, your understanding will be limited, but it can provide you with a foundation you can build upon at a later date.

For those of you who want more depth but still don't want to commit to reading the entire book, you can skim through the pages and read only the key concepts presented in *italics*. With even this minor amount of effort, you will still have learned more about money than most of your friends. Later, should you have an interest in any particular topic, you will have enough knowledge to skip directly to the appropriate chapter and fully understand its contents.

You might also want to look at the end of each chapter

for a *Practical App*. This information teaches you how to apply certain key concepts from that chapter in real-life situations, such as:

- How to open a checking account.
- How to check your credit report.
- What happens when you miss a credit card payment?
- How to spot tactics grocery stores use to get you to spend more money.
- Why you should never, ever give anyone else your debit card PIN.
- How to keep more of your money from your paycheck.

However, if you really want to take control of your money, you should read the entire book. You will find that most every topic is explored in depth. In fact, in the end, your understanding will probably exceed that of most adults.

28 money skills that will change your life

1. Understanding debt and when to use it.
2. When not to use debit cards.
3. Understanding credit scores and how to improve them.
4. Buying safely online.
5. Debt payments you should avoid.
6. Why you shouldn't use automatic withdrawal.
7. How to write a check.

27. Why you should say "no" to extended warranties.

28. Why you should exhaust government student loans before using private loans.

Master a powerful financial vocabulary

Also at the end of each chapter is a list of vocabulary words. If you see an unfamiliar word, you can easily go back and find its definition without looking through the whole book. Mastering these words is important so that you can understand the financial terms you will eventually encounter in credit card agreements, loan documents, and checking and savings accounts

What this book is not about

This is not a book for dummies. You are not a dummy. The fact that you are reading this book means you are smart enough to realize managing your money takes a certain amount of education. The more you know, the more your money can work for you. You work hard to earn it—why spend it without making every dime count?

You will not find any discussion about investing in this book, either. Although this is a very important topic, other than investing in a savings account, the majority of teens should probably avoid investing unless they have an experienced adult to guide them. Investing takes a thorough understanding of finance; otherwise, it is just gambling. In your teen years, you will be money ahead if you avoid borrowing instead of investing. So let's get started. Are you ready to reach for your dream.

* * *

Michael and Logan grew up in the same neighborhood, went to the same middle school and high school, and even played the same sports. Michael had always been better at school work, often getting all A's on his report card. Logan wasn't as smart as Michael, but he didn't envy him, either. He figured that's just the way of it. Logan also didn't work as hard as Michael, preferring to hang out with the guys instead.

Michael's parents made more money than Logan's, so Michael always had the latest phone and the flashiest running shoes. In high school, Michael even had his own car, a tricked-out Mustang with racing stripes.

It did bother Logan that his parents couldn't buy him the latest toys. If he wanted something, he had to get a job to buy it. He discovered quickly that toys are expensive, and he had to work a long time at minimum wage to afford them. His parents didn't give him a credit card either, so everything he bought had to be paid for out of his savings.

When it came time for college, Michael opted for an expensive private school and majored in English. He had set his heart on becoming a famous writer. Even Michael's parents couldn't afford to completely pay for tuition, so Michael borrowed the money — a lot of money. By the time he graduated, he owed over sixty thousand dollars, which he would have to begin to pay back just six months after graduation.

Logan chose the state university extension because the tuition was low and he could live with his parents for a couple of years, further reducing his expenses. He worked weekends and summers, and even then, he had to borrow about ten thousand dollars before he graduated. Logan decided on a career in teaching because he enjoyed working with kids. It also seemed like a career offering steady, long-term employment.

Michael never did become a writer, but he got a good-paying job in advertising. He was used to having nice things, which meant that between paying for them and repaying his school loans, he was constantly short of money. The minute he got a raise, he bought something expensive to reward himself. He worked hard at his job, often giving up weekends and holidays. In turn, he advanced and made more money. Unfortunately, he readily spent it to buy still more things to compensate for all the personal sacrifices his job required. His life had become his job, but at least he had a nice car and a nice apartment — he couldn't save enough to buy a house.

Logan, on the other hand, never made much money. He got a small raise every year, but working harder as a teacher didn't translate into more money. Like Michael, he had to pay off his college loan, but it wasn't nearly as large as Michael's, so it took him only five years to do it. Of course, he also couldn't afford a lot of nice things like Michael, but he had gotten used to living without them. Besides, his friends didn't have money either, so he didn't much care.

Logan did have one thing that Michael didn't have, and that was a plan. One day, the thought dawned on Logan that if he could pay off his student loan in five years, he could continue to make those same payments into his savings for the next five years. In the end, he would have ten thousand dollars, which he could use to buy a house. And so he did.

Next, he set his sights on a nice, used car, which he also paid for from savings. Then he built up his savings account for emergencies. After that, he bought new furniture, and, well, you get the idea. Because he only needed to cover a small house payment, Logan found he could finally afford to buy some fun things, like a new iPad and a big-screen TV.

Fast forward ten years. Michael is still working long hours. He's been through three layoffs, each requiring him to move to three different cities to find a replacement job. He misses his home town, but there isn't any work for him there. Each time he moves, he wipes out his meager savings. The rent for his apartment keeps going up, and his car is getting a little dated. But, he's still paying off the last one, so he can't afford a new one. He has no savings, and his credit rating is so poor he can't get a loan for a house, even if he could save enough for a down payment.

Meanwhile, Logan has had steady work with plenty of free time to hang out with his friends. He has his weekends free to do as he pleases and often spends them mountain biking, fishing, and playing the guitar. With almost no debt payments, except for his house, he has plenty of money to buy what he wants, including nice vacations. A couple of years ago he invested part of his savings in several growth stocks and quickly doubled his investment. Life is pretty good for Logan.

* * *

Now, the moral of this story is simply this: you don't need super smarts and an exclusive college education or even a high-paying job to afford the nicer things in life. All you need is to apply the very simple things you'll learn from this book. And, the magic of it is that anyone can do it—including you.

You've probably noticed that this is not a long book. That's because managing your money requires only understanding a few basic principles. Applying these principles is the hard part. But if you do, you'll be surprised at their power to change your life. Like Logan, you may not have been blessed with rich parents and a genius IQ, but that doesn't mean you can't come out a winner in the game of life. The fact that you are reading this book means you've got what it takes to succeed.

Money and Teens in a Nutshell

If you read nothing else in this book, read these four pages. They will give you the basics to better manage your money. Of course, you are encouraged to read all of the material in each chapter to get a complete understanding. None of this material is difficult to master. And in almost no time, you'll find that you will be spending smarter and saving more.

Chapter 1: Consumer Savvy

A savvy consumer understands the difference between needs and wants. Needs are expenses for shelter, food, education, transportation, and a job. Businesses use psychological tactics to make it harder to differentiate your wants from your needs. You can take control of your spending by recognizing these tactics and by using the many powerful tools found on the Internet, such as comparison shopping and customer reviews.

Chapter 2: Debt Savvy

Debt is an obligation from one person to another. A loan is a particular type of debt that involves money. The borrower is obligated to repay a loan to a lender, the one who lent the money, over some period of time in smaller amounts, called payments. The lender charges the borrower interest until the loan is repaid. This interest charge is added onto the total loan, which increases the amount of each payment.

Chapter 3: Banking Savvy

A checking account is a service provided by banks that keeps your money safe, while also giving you access to it as needed. You must first deposit, or place, your money into a checking account before you can spend it, either by writing a check or by using a debit card. Either way, you can only spend the amount you have deposited. Should you attempt to spend more, you will overdraw your account, incurring substantial fees and penalties.

Chapter 4: More About Debt

Unlike a debit card, each time you use a credit card, you are borrowing money. Credit cards carry a high interest rate, which results in a greater amount added onto your credit card loan. In turn, interest is then charged on both the original loan plus the interest charges. This *compounding of interest* can result in increasing the amount you owe several times over. Most credit cards offer a *grace period*. This is a period of time after you receive your credit card statement, which is free of interest charges for any purchases made during the previous month. You should strive to pay off your credit card before this grace period expires. Car loans and mortgages are loans which entitle the lender to reclaim some *collateral*, or property, from the borrower should the borrower fail to make timely payments.

Chapter 5: Credit Score Savvy

A credit score is a number between 300 and 850 (the higher the score the better) that is generated by a formula based upon all of the information in your credit report as compared with millions of others. Lenders use your score to predict how likely you are to manage your money responsibly. This score can affect every part of your life, including your future job prospects.

Chapter 6: Money Psychology

Your attitude toward money affects your savings and spending habits. Understanding your money attitudes helps you manage your money more successfully. Certain spending-related attitudes can lead you to carelessly waste your money, while other savings-related attitudes may prevent you from making worthwhile and necessary purchases.

Chapter 7: Your Financial Statement

A financial statement is a specific way to track the amount of money you earn and spend. If you spend more than you earn, you will have a negative bottom line. This means you have to borrow money or dip into savings to pay all your bills. Alternately, if you spend less than you earn, you will have a positive bottom line, allowing you to add to your savings. Tracking how you spend your money provides you with the information you need to spend it more wisely to achieve your financial goals.

Chapter 8: Budgeting Savvy

A budget is a road map, or a way to plan your financial future. Using the same format as the financial statement, a budget looks at the future—at what you intend to do with your money—as opposed to a financial statement which looks at your past. When you set up a budget, your first priorities should be to set up an emergency fund, pay down debt, and then *pay yourself first* (deposit money into your savings account before you spend it on anything else). You should compare your actual spending from your financial statement with your budget to help keep your spending on track.

Chapter 9: Checking Account Savvy

Filling out a paper check, recording checks in a check register, and balancing your checking account are basic skills you will use the rest of your life. A check register is an accounting form, either paper or electronic, that helps you keep track of the money in your checking account. One of its key uses is to help you avoid overdrafts, or writing checks for more money than you have deposited into your account. Overdrafts incur high penalty charges and can lower your credit score.

Chapter 10: Electronic Banking

Debit and credit cards, echecks, electronic funds transfers, and automatic withdrawal are all forms of electronic banking. Credit cards offer the strongest consumer protections, generally limiting your losses to fifty dollars if they are lost or stolen. Limit the use of your debit cards to withdrawing cash at ATMs and for small purchases. Do not use debit cards for online purchases. Avoid using automatic withdrawal, a type of prearranged bill payment, tied to your checking account.

Chapter 11: Tax Savvy

A tax is a financial charge levied by the government on individuals and property. Payment of taxes is not voluntary; rather, it is the responsibility of every United States citizen to pay for the goods and services provided by the government. The most common taxes include payroll taxes, sales taxes, income taxes, and property taxes.

Chapter 12: Compound Interest and Loans

Interest charges are expressed as an interest rate over some time period, such as one percent per month, or twelve percent per year. Simple interest is the interest charged on principal, as opposed to compound interest, which is the interest charged on principal, plus any previous, unpaid interest charges.

APR or Annual Percentage Rate restates interest charges in a consistent way so that you can meaningfully compare loans between different lenders. A secure loan means that the lender is entitled to take some property from the borrower, such as a car or boat, should the borrower fail to make timely payments. A collateralized loan will have a lower interest rate than a loan without collateral, such as a line of credit.

Chapter 13: Student Loan Savvy

Student loans can be either direct loans made by the government or loans from private lenders, such as Sallie Mae and banks. Some government loans are subsidized, such as subsidized Stafford Loans, meaning the government pays some of the loan costs in order to offer lower interest rates or more favorable repayment terms. Student loan payments begin after a short grace period following graduation and continue for ten to twenty-five years. A student loan is a serious obligation. This debt is very difficult to discharge through bankruptcy or other means to cancel the obligation.

1   Consumer Savvy

There are an endless number of books, blogs, and websites about saving money and smarter shopping. Rather than repeat some of this well-worn advice, some of which is obvious, let's look at a fundamental idea. If you want to save money, you have to spend less than you make. It's that simple. Don't be fooled by the thousand and one schemes concocted to avoid this simple truth. Even if your income increases, you can't increase your spending by the same amount, or you still won't save anything. Like most things in life; however, it's easy in concept but hard to do in practice.

Know your needs from your wants

Why? One reason is our very human failing to understand the difference between *needs* and *wants*. In our culture, we are bombarded with advertising designed to confuse the two. The need for one new pair of shoes turns into a need to have a pair to match every outfit in the closet. Or the need for a computer becomes the need for an iPad. If you are someone whose status is based upon what you own, you are particularly susceptible to these advertising ploys

> *A need arises from some basic requirement for food, shelter, transportation, education, or a job.*

Take the following simple quiz to help you decide if a purchase is a need or a want:

1. Am I buying this because all of my friends have it?
2. Am I buying this to impress others?
3. Am I buying this because I am bored?
4. Am I buying this without any thought?
5. Am I buying this to replace something that works just as well?
6. Am I buying this because I think it will change my life?
7. Am I buying this to keep up with the latest fashion?
8. Am I buying this because some advertisement has defined it as a need?
9. Am I buying this because I deserve it?
10. Am I buying this as an excuse to avoid doing something I should otherwise do?

If you answered yes to any of these questions, you are spending money on a *want* instead of a *need*. If you think about the questions above, they are either about satisfying some emotion tied to your self-esteem, or they are about adding some degree of excitement to your life. And, while these can be valid reasons to spend your money, you must recognize them for what they are. They are wants and not needs. Although satisfying your wants is the spice of life, too much of this can be unhealthy for your finances. Just as with your diet, you can eat chocolate cake or a thick, juicy steak, as long as you don't do it every day.

The trick to controlling your wants is to develop a habit of making your purchases a conscious effort, meaning that you take the time to think about why you want to buy something. If you can delay a purchase decision for at least twenty-four hours, or even longer for large purchases, you will have removed a great deal of the emotional excitement that may be driving you. In many cases, you'll find that after twenty-four hours, your level of interest will most likely have decreased.

Beyond this, you might want to think about other and better uses for your money, which you don't allow yourself to do when you thoughtlessly spend it. Once you start saving toward a goal, be it a car or college, your savings will begin to build a momentum of its own. Saving is like any habit: the more you do it, the easier it becomes.

Those dastardly retailers

When you begin to favor spending for your needs over your wants, you will still have a battle on your hands. In the last few years, businesses have become cleverer when it comes to luring you into spending more than you intend, even for basic needs. One way they do this (covered in more depth in *Chapter 3 Banking Accounts*) is with fees. However, fees aren't just limited to banking. Businesses seem to charge fees for everything: customer service, tech support, shipping and handling, cell phone usage, data plans, and on, and on. What's with all these fees? It's part of a strategy to conceal the tue cost of a product or service by *unbundling*, or taking what may have been part of a package and breaking it into smaller pieces, and then charging separately for each of those pieces.

These retailers are taking advantage of a psychological process called *anchoring*, in which consumers judge the value of one item by comparing its cost to an anchor cost. Consider a $60 per month cell phone plan. If you pay $10 in overages, this extra cost seems small compared to the larger $60 price anchor. If the basic plan cost $25, then the same overage charge would seem excessive. In addition, the overage charge allows the cell phone provider to keep the plan cost lower, so in turn, it appears better when compared to the competition.

The only way to win the battle of unbundling and fees is to take the time to read the fine print and be honest with yourself. If you use more cell phone time than allotted with the basic plan, then the advertised price is a fiction. You must include all the costs to make a valid comparison.

Extended warranties are your worst enemy

Extended warranties are another unbundled fee, covering your costs in case of product failure arising from a manufacturing defect. In this case, the cost of this warranty has been proven time and again to have almost no value, and, by all rights, it should be free as a part of the standard warranty. Retailers love this fee because it is almost pure profit for them, meaning it has almost no benefit to you.

A related trap to avoid plays on the reverse of unbundling. In this case, a business will offer a complete package, appropriately called a bundle, for one supposedly low price, in the hopes you will overpay for the complete package in order to avoid paying more for the extras. Free shipping works this way. Retailers offer you the opportunity to buy more in order to save shipping and handling costs. This can make sense, but only if you would have spent the required minimum in the first place. Otherwise, you are just spending money to avoid a fee. This can cost you as much, or more, than the costs you are trying to avoid.

Cable and phone companies are masters at bundling their services in order to make it more difficult for you to compare the pieces of their bundle individually. Once again, you have to take the time to look at what services you want, without all of the extras thrown in that have no value to you.

Incidentally, bundling isn't restricted to high tech purchases. Bagged salad is another example. Everything you need for a salad is bundled into one package. While the costs to buy the individual pieces — head lettuce, carrots, radishes, etc. — are a fraction of the bundled cost, consumers overlook this because it is difficult to calculate the cost of so many ingredients. This overload of ingredients appears to be a bargain because the sheer number of them counts for more psychologically than their actual amounts.

Use the Internet to fight back

You can defeat these retailer tactics by using the very powerful tools available on the Internet. Never before have there been more ways to shop for the best value. Through the Internet, you can access Facebook, forums, and customer reviews. Together these have dramatically increased your options for comparison shopping over any of those previously available, even a few years ago. However, you must make the effort and do your homework if you want to take advantage of them.

A major benefit of turning your purchases into a conscious effort is to allow you the time to make meaningful value comparisons among competing services and products. Read customer reviews before you buy. Check the fine print and make sure you understand what you are getting. If there is a long-term commitment involved, find out how much it will cost to end it, should the need arise. Many cell phone plans charge extraordinarily large financial penalties should you cancel their service before your contract with them ends. The time to understand this is *before* you sign their contract.

More consumer savvy advice

Want more consumer savvy advice? Avoid credit card debt. Credit card debt carries such high interest rates that you can easily find yourself in a hole from which you can never dig out. Instead of paying yourself first and saving money for your goals, you will be paying off credit card interest. In most cases, the interest you pay on your credit cards is money that offers you almost no benefit. Thousands and thousands of dollars are spent by consumers who use credit cards for their purchases because they want the privilege of having something a little sooner. Always ask yourself before you use your credit card: is this something I need to buy right away? Can it wait another week? Another month? The longer you wait to buy it, the longer you have to save for it and the more you will save in credit card interest charges.

Protect the most valuable thing you own

And speaking of credit cards, guard your credit as if it was the most valuable thing you own—because it is. Poor credit is like running against a fierce headwind. It can stop your progress toward your goals in its tracks. Poor credit affects everything from getting future credit to paying higher interest rates when you do. And in today's world, even employers will check your credit history before they offer you a job.

In this chapter, we have covered some of the basic concepts you can use to manage your money. Recognizing the tactics that retailers and others use to get you to spend more money is one critical tool you can use to make your dollars go further. Thanks to the Internet, powerful tools have been placed in your hands, like comparison shopping and consumer reviews.

Learn to use them before you buy. Finally, use credit wisely; it will dramatically improve your life .

Terms covered in Chapter 1

- **Wants**
- **Needs**
- **Bundle**
- **Unbundle**
- **Extended Warranty**
- **Anchoring**

Practical App: free shipping

The next time you are tempted to spend more money in order to take advantage of an offer for free shipping, ask yourself if you would have bought anything more without the offer. If the answer is no, then what you pay for that extra stuff is what the free shipping actually costs you. Yes, you did get something for the extra money, but if you didn't want it in the first place, what is it really worth? What could you have bought instead that would have been a better use of your money? This is called your opportunity cost, meaning once you spend your money for one thing, you can no longer spend it for another. So in a way, buying the first thing costs you the opportunity to buy something else. For example, ordering a hamburger for lunch costs you the opportunity to have a taco. Think about all of your spending this way. What could you have had instead? It is another psychological tool you can use to evaluate the true cost of any offer, like free shipping.

2 Debt Savvy

Understanding debt is as important as reading, writing, and arithmetic

If you want to successfully manage your money, you will first need to understand a few basic terms. There's no easy way to do this, except to memorize the definitions. It's like using your cell phone. You just have to memorize some things before you can make a call, like what do all those bars mean and where's the send button?

The same thing applies to your finances, and one of the most important of these terms is *debt*. Why start with debt? Because it is so readily available and failing to understand it leads to all sorts of problems in your life. So what exactly is debt?

A debt is an obligation owed by one person to another.

For example, if you borrow a book from the library, you have created a debt because you now owe the library the return of that book. In the terminology commonly used when referring to debt, the library is called the *creditor* and you are called the *debtor*.

Debt will be a part of the rest of your life

What is the difference between a debt and a loan?

A loan is a kind of debt for which money is owed by one person to another.

Loans also have their own vocabulary. For example, the creditor is called a *lender*, the debtor is called a *borrower*, and the amount of the loan is called the *principal*. Put another way, using these new terms:

A borrower borrows money from the lender, termed a loan, which is a debt or promise to pay the loan, or principal, back to the lender in the future.

Hold on a little longer, there are just a few more terms to go, but don't worry, you don't have to know all of these right away. Just as creditors are also called lenders, and debtors are also called borrowers, loans go by different names as well. Here are a few of the more common ones:

Credit Line	Mortgage
Payday Loan	Advance
Installment	Conventional
Overdraft	Collateralized

Why do we need all of these terms for the same thing? Why not call all loans by the same name? That would certainly make it easier to understand. However, lenders insist upon referring to debt by a very specific name because they want the borrower to know exactly how the money is to be used and how it will be paid back.

For example, a mortgage loan refers to a loan used to buy a house and is generally paid back over a long period of time, like fifteen to thirty years. On the other hand, a credit line refers to money borrowed by using a credit card, typically used to buy things found in a store or online, like televisions and iPhones. This type of loan is usually paid back over several months.

Regardless of what you call a loan, the borrower is still making a promise to repay the borrowed money to the lender in the future.

Whew! We're almost done with all these definitions.

No free lunches: payments and interest

Paying borrowed money back is done a little bit at a time in what are called *payments*. After a certain number of payments, you (as the borrower) will have returned all the borrowed money to the lender.

But wait! There's one final thing, and this is the most important thing to know about loans:

In addition to repaying the initial loan principal to the lender, the borrower also pays an extra amount of money called interest.

This extra amount is added on to each payment, and it is the reason a lender lends their money. These interest charges are the way the lender earns income. Interest charges keep banks in business. If they loaned out money and then got only that money back, they wouldn't have anything extra to pay the people who work for them.

The interest can be a lot or a little, and it is based upon

the type of loan and whether the lender believes that the borrower will repay it. We'll cover this in more detail later. For now you should remember these key points:

- A debt is an obligation owed by one person to another.
- A loan is a specific type of debt involving money.
- A loan must be repaid to the lender.
- A loan is paid back to the lender over time in smaller amounts, or payments.
- Each payment includes interest, which is additional money the lender charges the borrower until all the money is paid back.

* * *

Emily didn't understand why her parents couldn't afford to buy her the nice things her friends had, like an iPhone and expensive jeans. She knew her father had a good job; he was a manager at the local car dealership.

They did have a nice, new car. In fact, they had two really nice cars that were only a couple of years old. Her mom's car was her favorite. It had leather seats and a killer stereo system. Every once in a while, when her mom wasn't around, she'd sneak into the garage and plug in her iPod to listen to her favorite tunes on it.

Sometimes, a letter would come in the mail and then her dad and mom would get into a fight about the cars.

They fought over something called payments, but she didn't understand what that meant. She did know that those payments had something to do with money. She knew this because whenever she asked to buy something at the store, her mother would frown and tell her that they couldn't afford it because of those payments.

Then, one day her father lost his job. Now her parents had even less money. Emily, in turn, had to make do with even fewer toys and clothes. Those letters in the mail became more frequent until one day they suddenly stopped. At about the same time, Emily went out to the garage to plug her iPod into the car stereo and discovered the car was gone.

When she asked her mother what had happened to the car, her mother looked away and said they couldn't afford the car payments anymore. Emily thought about that for the longest time. It seemed to her that things wouldn't be so bad if it weren't for those payments.

So right then, she promised herself that whatever payments were, she'd never, ever have any of her own.

* * *

Terms covered in Chapter 2

- **Debt**
- **Borrower**
- **Payment**
- **Interest Rate**
- **Loan**
- **Lender**
- **Principal**
- **Creditor**
- **Debtor**

Practical App: credit card interest

Want to see how interest charges affect loan costs? Look at the following example for a credit card loan of $1,000, repaid in eighteen equal, monthly payments (one and a half years). The first row shows the monthly and total payment amounts without interest, while the second row includes a typical credit card interest charge of 12 percent per year.

Exhibit 2.1 interest charges for 18 months

	Monthly Payment	Total After 18 Months
Monthly payment without interest	$55.56	$1,000.00
Monthly payment with 12% interest	$60.98	$1,097.64
Difference	**$5.42**	**$97.64**

As you can see, interest charges have added $5.42 onto each payment resulting in a total of $97.64 in additional charges over the life of the loan. Now, let's see what happens if we take twice as long (36 months) to repay this same loan:

Exhibit 2.2 interest charges for 36 months

	Monthly Payment	**Total After 36 Months**
Monthly payment without interest	$27.77	$1,000.00
Monthly payment with 12% interest	$33.21	$1,195.56
Difference	**$5.44**	**$195.56**

Although, increasing the number of payments hasn't significantly increased the monthly payment amount, look at what happens to the total difference paid. It has doubled from $97.64 to $195.56. This leads us to a basic rule that you can apply to all loans:

If you take longer to pay off a loan, more of your money will go toward paying interest charges.

The greater the interest rate, the more this is true. Because of this basic fact, always try to pay *higher* interest rate loans off more quickly than those with lower interest rates.

3 Banking Savvy

Money in your pocket, wallet, or even in a shoe box is called *cash*. In the United States, cash is accepted by everyone, whenever and wherever money is required. It can be used to pay for anything from groceries, to utilities, to loan payments.

Carrying a lot of cash around with you, however, is inconvenient and might even be dangerous. As you know, someone who steals your cash can use it with complete confidence that others will accept it without question. And, if you should lose your cash, you will be out of luck to get it back. In order to avoid these risks, banking was invented as a safe place to keep your cash, while still allowing you to use it as needed.

Keeping your money safe

You can *deposit*, or place, your cash in a bank in several different types of accounts, depending upon how you wish to use your cash in the future.

> *A bank account is an agreement between you and the bank, allowing the bank to use your money until you ask for it back. You can ask for it back whenever you want, or make demand for it, in a number of convenient ways.*

It all starts with a checking account

A checking account is one of the most common types of bank accounts, providing a convenient means to retrieve your money from the bank, simply by writing a paper check. However, a check is not the same as cash. When you buy something with a check, like a pair of running shoes, you are in essence asking the shoe store to trust that they can exchange your check for cash sometime in the future. Until the store has that cash, they are relying on your promise.

A check is only a promise of future payment until it is funded by money from your checking account.

With a basic checking account you can write checks only until all of the money you have deposited is *withdrawn*, or used up. At that point, the bank will refuse to exchange cash for any more of your checks. Intentionally writing checks for more money than you have in your checking account is a crime. Whether intentional or otherwise, both the store holding your check and your bank will take a dim view of your broken promise and at the very least will charge you large penalty fees. They will also require you to make good on your promise by requiring you to deposit money into your checking account to *cover*, or pay, for the check you wrote.

* * *

It was a dark and stormy night. No, really. Madison's parents were out for the evening, and she was getting nervous. They had promised her they would be back in time to take her to the mall. The school dance was the next day, and she desperately needed a new pair of shoes to match her new dress.

She texted them several times, but she hadn't received a word in return. She had asked them to take her shopping earlier in the week, but the time slipped by because of one thing or another. Now time had run out.

She just couldn't imagine going to the dance without a complete outfit. This was the biggest dance of the spring semester. How could she face Blake, her dream date? Every time she thought about him, her knees went weak.

She had to do something. Maybe her friend Calee could help. She frantically punched the speed dial on her phone.

"Hello, Calee? . . . No, nothing yet. . . . I don't know. . . . They said they'd be home in time, and now it's already 8:30. . . . Yeah, I know. . . . I know. . . . I know."

Long pause.

"Hey, could you give me a ride? I'll never ask for anything else ever. . . . I promise."

Click.

Ten minutes later Calee arrived at the front door. "Maddy? You there?"

"Oh, thank God," said Maddy as she flung the front door open. "Calee, you're a life saver. Let's get to the store."

"But Maddy, haven't you forgotten something? What are you going to do for money?"

"I'll have to write a check and work it out later."

"Your parents aren't going to like that."

"I know, but I don't have a choice."

"Maddy, this is so not a good idea. If you write another bad check, you'll be grounded, for like, a year."

"I'll take my chances."

Two hours later...

"Okay girls, will that be all?" asked the store clerk.

"Yes, please," replied Maddy as she handed over the bright red pair of high heels.

"That comes to eight-five dollars and sixty-four cents with tax."

Maddy pasted on her biggest smile as she handed the check to the clerk. The clerk scanned the check through the register. A frown crossed her face.

"Excuse me a minute," said the clerk as she nervously eyed the two girls. She disappeared into the back of the store for the longest time.

Beads of perspiration broke out on Maddy's forehead. A few minutes later, the clerk reappeared with an older man dressed in a charcoal suit. Maddy's head swam and her stomach tightened into a knot.

The man walked over to her and stared down. Maddy took a step back.

"Excuse me miss, but there seems to be a problem with your check."

Maddy froze. The man's icy stare bore right through her. She could barely keep from fainting.

Maybe there are worse things than not having the right pair of shoes, she thought.

* * *

A very bad idea: overdrawing your checking account

Writing a bad check, or a check for which there isn't enough money in your checking account to cover it, is a big problem for banks. Many people write bad checks accidentally because they don't keep good records. But, some people write bad checks on purpose, in the hopes of tricking others into giving them money or something else of value, and getting away before they are caught.

Writing a bad check, as Maddy found out, is a bad idea. At a minimum, you will pile up a lot of charges to cover everyone else's inconvenience, and you will most likely find your checking account shut down. The best advice is to never do it. Ever. Later you'll learn to keep a record of your checks so that you won't do it accidentally.

What you need to know about debit cards

Another way you can spend the money in your checking account is with a debit card. A debit card is like an electronic check. Instead of filling out and signing a paper form, you swipe a debit card through a card reader. When you use a debit card to buy something at a store, for example, the store is again accepting your promise that when your debit card charge reaches your bank, you will have the money in your account to cover the charge. Debit cards are more convenient to use than paper checks because there isn't any paperwork. This also means money is withdrawn much more quickly from your account.

> *A debit card withdraws money from your checking account, like a paper check, but it is not the same as a paper check, and there are other differences which are important to understand.*

We will cover those differences later. For now, just remember that a debit card withdraws money from your checking account.

In the last few years banks have invented a number of other ways for you to retrieve money from your checking account without writing a paper check, such as electronic funds transfers and automatic payments. Most of these have come about as a way to avoid handling paper. However, just as with a debit card, these other ways are not the same as writing a paper check.

A savings account your ticket to the future

A savings account is a bank account with which most everyone is familiar.

A savings account is an agreement between you and the bank that places certain restrictions on how you can withdraw your money. In turn, the bank pays you interest for this restriction.

Typically, when you have a savings account, you are required to visit your bank to make a withdrawal, making it less convenient than a checking account. In essence, a savings account is a loan you make to the bank. The bank pays you interest for the privilege of borrowing your money to use for their purposes, just as you pay them interest if you borrow money from them. When you deposit money into a bank savings account, you are now the lender, and the bank is the borrower.

As you will recall, a bank adds interest charges to your loan payments so that they can pay the costs for their employees and offices. When you have a savings account, you have become the bank. You are now earning that same money for yourself. And the best part is that you don't have to lift a finger to get it. By simply depositing your money into a savings account, you make money every day you leave it there.

Earn more: certificates of deposit

Generally, you can demand any of your money back

from a savings account at any time. Obviously, banks would like to keep your money for as long as they can so that they, in turn, can lend it out and make more interest income. To encourage you to keep your money in your savings account for a longer period of time, they will offer to pay you more interest. A *CD*, or *Certificate of Deposit*, is one such way you can earn more interest in exchange for your commitment not to withdraw your money.

A CD can be for any amount of money and for any length of time, from a month to years. The longer you commit to leaving your money in the CD, the greater the interest you can earn. However, if you withdraw your money before the agreed upon time, the bank will not pay you as much interest as initially agreed upon. In addition, they may charge you a penalty.

In this chapter, we have covered some of the more common types of bank accounts, including some of the ways you can withdraw money from those accounts, such as paper checks and debit cards. People use bank accounts to avoid the risks and hassles of carrying cash.

If you have cash that you will not need until some time in the future, you can keep it in a savings account until you do need of it. Banks pay you interest for keeping your money in a savings account. The longer you keep it in a savings account, the more they will pay you.

Terms covered in Chapter 3

- **Cash**
- **Checking Account**
- **Paper Check**
- **Checking account**
- **Debit Card**
- **Certificate of Deposit**

Practical App: opening a checking account

Opening a checking account at a bank is a straightforward process. Here is a list of steps:

To get started, decide how much money you will deposit into your checking account.

1. Shop around for checking accounts with the lowest fees. Local banks and credit unions are good places to begin. Don't look at only the monthly maintenance fee. Take into account all of the other fees for such things as overdrafts, customer service, etc.

2. You will need to fill out an application asking for your name, birth date, and social security number, along with other personal information. After reading the checking account terms describing your responsibilities, along with those of the bank, you and your parents (if you are under 18) will need to agree to those terms and sign the application.

3. In most cases, the bank will provide you with some temporary paper checks to use at first, but you will have to purchase more. You will also

need to decide whether you want a debit card tied to your account.

4. The bank may take a few days to approve your application and set up your account.

5. Congratulations. Once the bank establishes your checking account, you may begin spending your money by either using your debit card or writing a temporary check.

4 More About Debt

In this chapter, we'll look at debt in a little more detail. As you recall from Chapter 2, debt is an obligation of one person, or debtor, to another, or creditor. And, a loan is a kind of debt involving money.

Loans come in many varieties. One of the most common is a *credit card line*, or *revolving credit*, which is a loan created automatically when you use a credit card and where the initial loan amount can increase or decrease during the life of the loan.

Credit cards and noses: everybody has one

Just like debit cards, credit cards are used to make purchases by swiping them through an electronic reader; however, credit cards and debit cards work differently.

> *A debit card uses money you have deposited into your checking account, while a credit card uses money that banks or other credit-card lenders loan to you.*

Every time you use a credit card, you are borrowing money you will have to repay. Banks aren't the only ones who offer credit cards. Other *card issuers* include major retailers like Sears and Macy's, and energy companies like Exxon and Chevron.

Why do they do this? These non-bank credit card issuers use credit cards as a way to encourage their customers to buy more of their products through discounts, customer loyalty rewards, and higher credit card limits. Like banks, they also earn interest from the credit card loans they make to their customers.

Amazing grace period

Credit cards often offer another unique feature. When you use a credit card, the money you borrow is free of interest as long as it is paid back within a certain period of time called a *grace period*. This interest-free period generally runs from twenty to twenty-five days after the credit card issuer sends you a statement. A statement is a detailed accounting of your card usage from the previous month. Grace periods do not apply to credit card charges you make prior to your last statement. In other words, if you do not pay off all of your credit card charges from the previous month, any charges left over will have interest added to them.

A grace period is a period of time beginning from the time you receive your credit card statement, during which you can pay off the charges from the previous month without paying any interest.

This is one of the greatest benefits credit cards offer. In essence, you can use your credit card without cost (provided that you pay it off before the grace period ends.) It's like a free loan from the bank. Why do credit card issuers do this? Because they know that people will charge more on their cards, believing they will pay them off before the grace period expires, but in the end, most will not. Not all cards have a grace period, so you should choose only the ones that do.

Slow poison: minimum credit card payments

If you do not pay the amount you owe on the card within the grace period, you then have to make at least some minimum payment every month until you do. The card issuer determines this minimum amount, which includes both interest and a portion of the *balance*, or the amount you borrowed. In some cases, this balance can be transferred to another card. Essentially, you are using the money you borrow from a new credit card to pay off the balance from another. The reason you might want to do this is that the new credit card might offer lower interest charges on your transferred balance.

Card issuers often offer incentives, such as lower interest rates, to reward balance transfers as a way to get you to switch to their card. Be aware though, there is typically no grace period for balance transfers, meaning interest charges are applied immediately.

Because credit cards rely only on your promise to pay off your debt, the interest charges are generally quite high. This means each payment includes a very high, extra amount to cover interest charges. How much? Let's say you have a $100 balance on your card and you plan to pay it off in equal payments of $10 per month. With interest charges included, instead of ten months ($10 per month times 10 months = $100), it will actually take eleven months. So you wind up paying a total of $110 in order to pay off your original $100 balance.

Paying an extra $10 over a year's time for the privilege of having $100 to spend right away may not sound like such a bad deal. However, watch what happens when the balance is $1,000, but you still only pay $10 per month.

If you make monthly payments of $10 on a credit card balance of $1,000, you will never pay it off, no matter how many payments you make. Ever.

Shocked? How can this be? Because the interest charges on the $1,000 are equal to your monthly payment. Even if you double your monthly payment to $20 per month, it will still take you approximately six years to pay it off in full. In the end, you will pay $400 in interest charges or a third more than the total amount of money you borrowed in the first place. That $1,000 will cost you $1,400. Still sound like a great deal?

Credit card debt is one of the fastest ways to get into trouble. Credit card companies are happy to let you keep borrowing because the interest charges can add up so rapidly, especially if you make small monthly payments.

If you don't pay at least the interest charges for each month, those charges are added onto your credit card balance, which results in interest charges on interest charges.

Paying interest on interest leads to a financial wreck. It's worse than running in place. You make payments, but the amount you owe keeps increasing. This is called compounding. Albert Einstein once called it the most powerful force in the universe. Most people who use credit cards do not realize this until it is too late. At some point, the original balance becomes so large that they simply cannot make any headway at all.

The loan that ate my car: installment loans

Another common type of loan goes by the name of *installment credit,* which is a loan made for a specific purpose with fixed payments extending for a fixed amount of time. A *car loan* is a good example. All of the money is loaned once at the start, to be used only to buy a car or other vehicle. This money cannot be used to shop at the mall or to buy things from Amazon.com. The *loan term,* or number of payments, is locked in up front, and the interest payments are usually lower than for credit card debt. Why? Because the bank or other lender has the right to take your car should you fail to live up to your promise to pay back the loan.

When a lender makes a car loan, they have the right to take the borrower's car and to sell it to help pay off the debt, should the borrower fail to make timely payments.

If the lender can't sell the vehicle for a sufficient amount of money, the borrower is still required to make payments until the lender is fully repaid. Failure to make good on a car loan could result in a borrower making payments for a car he or she no longer even owns.

Mortgages

Still another familiar type of installment loan is a *mortgage*. The collateral in this case is real estate or other property, like a house, building, or even land. The loan term is usually much longer than for a car loan or a credit card loan, extending fifteen to thirty years or more. The interest rates are typically less than for other types of installment debt because property does not tend to lose value like a car or a boat. The lender, therefore, stands a better chance to get back its money, should the borrower fail to make repayment.

Prior to making a mortgage, the bank will get an expert opinion, called an *appraisal*, as to the worth of the property. As extra insurance, most lenders will not lend an amount equal to the full value of the real estate. The difference between full value and the loan amount is called the *loan to value ratio*. For example, if a piece of property is worth $1,000, the bank might lend a maximum of $800, which is an 800 / 1000 ratio or an 80 percent loan to value. In some cases, the bank may only lend $500, equating to a 500 / 1000 ratio, or a 50 percent loan to value.

Where does the rest of the money come from to buy the property? You, the borrower, have to use your cash, called a *down payment*, to make up the difference. In the above example, for a loan to value ratio of 80 percent, the down payment would be equal to 20 percent of the $1,000, or $200.

Borrowers must contribute their own money to make up the difference between the amount of money that a lender will loan for real estate and the purchase price.

At one time, lenders were willing to lend nearly 100 percent of the real estate value. Consequently, buyers only needed to come up with a very small down payment, mostly to cover loan fees. Lenders did this because they thought that the real estate would always go up in value. They believed they could get their money back if the borrowers failed to make good on the loan repayment. Instead, real estate values fell, and the borrowers had so little of their cash invested that many simply walked away, leaving the banks to do the best they could to sell the property. Few lenders, however, ended up covering the entire cost of their loans. When a borrower *defaults*, or fails to meet their loan obligations, they are making a very serious decision which will impact them well into the future. In some cases, they may not be able to get a loan for anything for a long period of time.

The penalty box: loan default

Finally, for every loan we have covered, and most others as well, there is some penalty when the borrower fails to make payments on time and in the required amounts. At a minimum, Lenders will often add fees ranging from $25 to $50 or more onto each late payment. If the borrower then fails to make other payments on time, the lender will add even more fees and will sometimes increase the interest rate as well.

Learning to use the proper amount of debt and to use it for the right reasons is the heart and soul of good money management. Understanding the simple concepts presented in this chapter is just the beginning. When you borrow money, you are committing a portion of your future earnings so that you can purchase something today. In the end, many borrowers may commit so much of their future earnings that they can no longer afford even their basic living expenses. As a result, they are penalized in many ways, which we will discuss in the next chapter.

Terms overed in Chapter 4

- **Credit Card Debt**
- **Grace Period**
- **Compound Interest**
- **Collateral**
- **Car Loan**
- **Mortgage**
- **Appraisal**
- **Down Payment**
- **Loan Default**

Practical App: late payments

Uh-oh. You missed one of your credit card payments. Here's what you can expect will happen:

The credit card issuer will charge you a late fee of up to

$35. However, thanks to new laws, this fee will be no more than the amount of your minimum payment.

1. If you are more than sixty days late, your interest rate will be raised to the highest rate allowed for any new charges to your card, greatly increasing your future borrowing costs.

2. The card issuer may report your late payment to a credit bureau, negatively impacting your credit score. Your credit score is a report card on your finances that follows you for the rest of your life. It will affect whether or not you can borrow money with acceptable terms and interest rates.

3. Should you make a payment, but for less than the minimum, you will not avoid any of the above penalties.

If you must delay making a payment, the best thing to do is to make the minimum payment as soon as possible. If you have a good track record, you may be able to call your bank, or other credit card issuer, and have your late fees waived. The best advice is to have an emergency fund so that you never miss a credit card payment.

5 Credit Score Savvy

Things were looking up for Christopher. After a long search, he had finally landed a summer job, and it even paid more than minimum wage. His friends were envious — most had given up looking long before. But Christopher happened to be at the right place at the right time when a friend of his dad's was looking for summer help.

Now he needed a car to get to work. It was too far to ride a bike; besides, it was a hassle to pedal through busy traffic twice a day to and from his job. He couldn't afford much, just about anything reliable would do. His dad offered to help him pay some of the cost. For the rest, he would have to get a loan.

He knew a little something about loans because he had a credit card. Every month, the bank sent him a statement showing him how much he had charged on his card and how much he needed to pay. His parents had given him the card trusting him to handle it wisely. In fact, they never asked to see what he bought as long as he made the payments.

Most months, he managed to make his payments on time, but on occasion, he came up short. The bank charged him a late fee of $35 each time, and his interest rate had been increased by half again from 12 percent to 18 percent per year. As a result, his minimum payments had more than doubled, so he was glad he had found a job. Just as soon as he got his first paycheck, he would put his finances back on track.

The next day, Christopher and his dad went car shopping. They must have looked at over a hundred cars, everything from a red, 1995 Toyota Corolla to a green, 1996 Audi A4. They finally settled on a very used, 2001 Subaru Outback. It had a few dents and about 150,000 miles, but it started right up and the tires looked okay.

Christopher figured that with his dad's help, he would only need to borrow about $3,000 to buy it. If everything went according to plan, he could just afford his monthly car payments along with insurance, gas, and, oh yes, those pesky credit card payments. He had to pinch himself. He was finally getting his own car. No more borrowing the family mini-van.

Christopher dressed up in his navy sports jacket and freshly ironed tie. Together with his father, they headed downtown to meet with the loan officer at the bank. It made him feel like a grown-up, knowing this meeting would be about *his* loan for *his* new car.

Mr. Needles, a balding man in his late forties, came out to meet them. He escorted them back to his office, all the while pointing out the new improvements in the bank lobby. He spent a few minutes telling them about the type of loan he thought best fit Christopher's needs and how the bank's rates were as good as or better than any other bank in town. Christopher didn't understand a lot of what Mr. Needles talked about as he droned on about things like APRs, fees, payment options, and penalties. Frankly, all Christopher wanted was the money. The rest didn't much matter.

At last, Christopher's father said he was satisfied with the loan terms and told Mr. Needles to start the paperwork. Because this was to be Christopher's loan, he provided most of the information, including his social security number, date of birth, and some details about his new job.

Mr. Needles scooped up the loan application and disappeared around the corner without a further word. Christopher eyed his dad nervously. He hadn't mentioned his late credit card payments. He was relieved that the loan officer hadn't asked. Drumming his fingers on the armrest of his chair, Christopher took deep breaths to keep from passing out.

After an eternity, Mr. Needles reappeared, taking a seat behind the desk. He had a frown on his face as he riffled through several papers. Finally, he glanced up.

"I'm afraid there's a problem with Christopher's credit." Mr. Needles tapped the papers in front of him. "According to this report, his credit score is . . . well . . . it doesn't meet the bank's requirements."

Christopher's jaw dropped. He saw his car and his plans go up in smoke before his eyes.

"There must be some mistake," Christopher's dad stated in an indignant tone.

"I'm afraid not," replied Mr. Needles. "It says here he has missed a number of payments on this credit card, and the balance is pretty big, too. His credit score is just too low for the bank to make him a loan." Mr. Needles delivered this news with as little emotion as if he had just read the weather forecast.

Christopher's dad turned to look at Christopher. "Is what he said true?"

Christopher stared down at his freshly-polished dress shoes. Without looking up, he nodded his head.

Christopher's dad turned back to face Mr. Needles. "We're sorry we wasted your time."

And with that, Christopher and his dad got up and walked back into the lobby. Neither of them spoke, but Christopher felt the weight of his father's disappointment on him. He had wanted to show his father that he could handle adult responsibilities. Now, he had only proven himself inadequate to the challenge.

Being an adult was going to be a lot harder than he thought.

*　*　*

Putting points on the scoreboard: credit scores

Whether you like it or not, there are certain things that will always be a part of your life, like your date of birth, social security number, where and when you graduated from high school, and your *credit score*.

Credit scores are like your high school grade point average except instead of measuring how well you do in school, they tell how well you manage your money.

Almost without exception, whenever you apply for a loan or a credit card, your credit score will factor into whether or not you will be approved and what terms you will be offered. Credit scores are now used as a prerequisite should you wish to rent an apartment or even when you apply for a job. A growing number of employers believe that if you can't manage your money, you can't manage a job either.

In the twenty-first century, your credit score will impact every part of your adult life.

Everything from buying a car, as Christopher discovered, to your employment, to paying for college, to buying a house can hinge on your credit score. Is this fair? Probably not, but it is a fact. And because it is a fact of modern life, you should understand what a credit score is and how you can ensure that it works for you—not against you.

Understand the credit score components

A credit score is a number between 300 and 850 (the higher the better) that is generated by a formula developed by *FICO*, or Fair Isaac and Company, based upon a comparison of the information in your credit report to millions of others. The FICO software then predicts how likely you are to manage your money responsibly. The formula includes not only your loan payment history, but also how well you have handled paying all of your bills; everything from how timely you have paid your cell phone bill to your monthly rent payments can find its way into your credit report.

There are three major credit reporting bureaus that track all of your financial information: Equifax, TransUnion, and Experian. These credit bureaus provide the raw credit data used in the FICO credit scoring formula. The formula assigns a degree of importance to each kind of credit information by using a percentage to arrive at a weighted average. For example, in the hypothetical formula below, credit information A and B are weighted equally because they each account for one-half of the final score.

$$A (50\%) + B (50\%) = \text{Credit Score} (100\%)$$

In the next formula, the different types of information are weighted differently, but in total they still add up to 100 percent of the credit score.

$$A (25\%) + B (25\%) + C (50\%) = \text{Credit Score} (100\%)$$

As you can see, in the second formula the weight, or importance, of A and B, which accounted for 50 percent each in the first formula, have now been reduced to half of their former weights, and C now makes up the other half.

In the FICO credit-scoring formula, the types of

information, or components, and their weighting, or degree of importance, are as follows::

Component	Weighting
How well you pay your bills	35%
How much money you owe and how much you can borrow	30%
How long you have had credit	15%
Your mix of credit—revolving and installment loans	10%
How many credit applications you have recently made	10%
Your Total Credit Score	100%

Let's look at each of these components individually.

Component 1: Paying your bills means how often you have paid your bills on time and for the full amount. If the cell phone bill is due on the first of the month and you pay it on the fifteenth or even a month later, you may find this information in your credit report. Your payment history for credit card payments, installment loan payments, and mortgages will almost certainly be included.

Component 2: How much you owe and how much you can borrow refers to the total amount of your outstanding debt, including credit cards, car loans, installment debt, cash advances, and mortgages. The more you owe as compared with others with the same income as yourself, the lower your score will be. If you have a $30,000 loan for a car and you work at a near-minimum-wage job, you most likely will be denied further credit.

This component also takes into account how much credit you might use in the future. For example, credit card issuers place a maximum limit on the amount of money you can borrow with their card. In some cases, this limit may be quite high. You might be granted a $5,000 maximum even though you routinely use $1,000. If you have a number of credit cards with high maximum limits, you would then have the potential to borrow $15,000 or even $20,000. This potential debt concerns lenders because they have found, through hard experience, that those with access to credit often use it at some time in the future. This creates the very real risk that the borrower won't be able to pay it all back. Recall the discussion on credit card debt in Chapter 3. The potential to access significant amounts of debt will negatively impact your credit card score.

Component 3: How long you have had credit captures your experience with managing credit. Someone who has never had to make payments poses a greater risk than someone who has proven that they can make their payments on time. Past behavior is a fairly reliable predictor of future behavior.

Component 4: Mix of credit looks at your experience with various types of credit, such as revolving credit, installment debt, student loans, and mortgages, to mention a few. Those who have managed all of these types of debts will have a higher ranking for this component.

Component 5: Number of credit applications tracks the number of times you have applied for credit in the recent past. Lenders believe those who have been actively looking for more credit may be facing some immediate financial need, perhaps stemming from the loss of a job or some financial setback. However, this component is adjusted to account for someone who is shopping around for the best credit deal, such as a credit card with a low interest rate.

The weighting, or importance, of each of the components indicates that in the FICO formula, *Component 1: Paying your bills and Component 2: How much you owe*, are by far the most important factors. This only makes sense. Lenders want to lend to those who have demonstrated they can live up to their obligations. Borrowers' promises to pay back their loans need to be believable. On the other hand, Component 2 assures lenders that borrowers don't have so much debt that they can't meet their obligations, even if they wanted to do so.

Taming your credit score

Credit scores are so important that there is an entire industry devoted to helping people manage and improve their credit scores. However, their advice amounts to much of the same thing. Understand all loan terms before you borrow money, and don't borrow unless you are certain you can meet those terms. Loan terms include, among other things, how the borrowed money will be used, how it will be paid back, and the penalties if you should fail to comply with those terms.

Here are some other ways to improve your score. Don't apply for more credit than you need. As explained in Component 5, this additional credit can hurt your score.

Also, be sure to make your loan payments a priority over all your other bills. Your payment history for these obligations will almost certainly end up in your credit score.

Borrowing must be taken seriously. Failing to live up to your promises can adversely impact your life. As Christopher discovered, he may well lose his summer job, along with the career potential it might have afforded him.

In the next chapter we will look at how you can manage debt intelligently, with an eye on getting what you want today without sacrificing your future to have it.

In this chapter we covered the basic components of the FICO credit score. It is a number that lenders, landlords, and even future employers use to make decisions about you. It is a number that will follow you for the rest of your life.

Terms covered in Chapter 5

- **Credit Score**
- **Credit Components**
- **Weighting**
- **Credit Bureaus**
- **Debt Terms**
- **FICO**

Practical App: reviewing your credit report

Take the time to review your credit reports at least once a year. AnnualCreditReport.com is the only authorized source that is free by law. You can fill out an application to receive a report once per year from each of the three nationwide credit reporting companies: Experian, Equifax, and TransUnion.

After you receive your report, you should look for unfamiliar accounts or any inaccurate information. You will want to call the reporting agency as soon as possible to dispute any inaccuracies you find.

6 Money Psychology

Saving? Spending? It seems as though there is a cosmic battle between the forces of spenders, who can't hang on to their money, and savers, who can't let go of it.

Here is what some young adults have to say about their attitudes toward money:

> "Money, Money Money. I love earning money. Money is very important to me because I like to do many things that cost a whole lot. I don't like asking my parents for money, or anyone else for that matter. So I earn it my own way."

> "I know how to save money; I'm just really, really bad at it."

> "When I spend my money, I feel really guilty afterwards, and I feel like I didn't really need whatever I bought."

> "I hate money. It makes people greedy and causes them to lose sight of what is important in life."

> — Your Attitudes Toward Money – comments NY Times Learning Network Blog

Money with an attitude

Recognize yourself in any of these comments? Thanks to research in the emerging field of behavioral economics, or the study of money and psychology, we now have a better understanding of how attitudes and personalities affect the way people manage their money.

In a recent book, *It's Not About the Money*, financial planner Brent Kessel identifies eight distinct types of money personalities, ranging from *The Innocent*, who don't attend to their money, believing instead everything will eventually work out; to *The Saver*, who derive feelings of abundance and a sense of self worth from their money; to *The Star*, who spends money to attract attention and impress others. Each of these money personalities views money differently. Kessel then makes the argument that you must first understand your money personality before you can effectively manage your money.

Along a similar vein, Brad Klontz, in an article in the *Journal of Financial Therapy*, identifies the following four typical money attitudes, or scripts, as he refers to them:

Money Avoidance:	a belief that money is bad
Money Worship:	a belief that money will solve all problem
MoneyStatus:	a belief that money is a status symbol
Money Vigilance:	the classic miser

Of course, few people fit neatly into any one category all of the time, but for most, one of the above probably represents a dominant money personality or attitude.

Financial planners, psychologists, and economists have found that uncovering subconscious beliefs about money and bringing them to the conscious empowers individuals to make better money choices. This new thinking parallels similar advances in education and medicine. All of these disciplines are moving toward a more customized approach, recognizing that advice and guidance must take into account individual differences to be effective.

Of course, at the most basic level, managing your money is a choice between saving and spending. If you want things like iPods, shoes, and video games more than money, then you spend. Conversely, if you want money more than the things it can buy, then you save. However, the two are not at odds with one another; rather, they are part of a spending/saving cycle. For example, you can save money with the goal of eventually spending it, or spend it with the goal of eventually saving it. We'll examine this closer in a moment.

Everyone will make literally thousands of decisions to spend or save throughout their lifetime. Psychologists tell us that some feel better having money, while others feel better about having the things it can buy. The point of their research is to uncover the hidden or subconscious reasons that underlie the choice to spend or save in order to help people make those choices which result in happier and healthier outcomes.

* * *

Jordan awoke with a start. She could remember desperately trying to sleep at four in the morning. At every attempt, her heart would start pounding as she lay there trying to calm herself. Finally, she managed to drift off, and now she had overslept. If she scrambled, she could make it to first period before the late bell. Just.

She couldn't believe today had finally arrived. Her high school team was headed for the state lacrosse finals. And even if they didn't win, she still had a university athletic scholarship — something she couldn't have imagined only a couple of years before. She found her thoughts flashing back to those times. Her life certainly hadn't turned out the way she had imagined it then.

In those days, Jordan had loved to shop. She lived to shop. When she wasn't shopping, she was planning her next trip to the mall or the second-hand store downtown, the one with the vintage clothing. She liked to dress up in silk and lace, like a Victorian lady.

She also treated her friends to Starbucks several times a week, which made her very popular. She even bought an occasional latte for her geography teacher. Sometimes, she wondered if that was why everyone liked her, then she'd brush the thought away. Instead, she told herself she just had a natural gift for attracting friends into her life.

She loved to show her friends her latest outfits and other things she brought back from her shopping trips, like a color e-Reader, or a stunning pair of pink, high-heel shoes. She could see the look of envy on her friends' faces, and she loved every minute of it.

Sometimes, she'd run out of money early in the month, forcing her to wait for a couple weeks until her parents gave her more. She had a very generous allowance, but even that didn't cover all her expensive purchases. When she did run out of money, she'd either hit up her parents, or at the very worst, she would lay low, claiming she had homework to do, or she would cook up some other excuse as a cover.

As soon as a new month rolled around, she'd splurge to make up for lost time. At her favorite stores, they knew her by name. She considered most of the sales ladies to be her friends.

Then one day, her world came crashing down. Her parents divorced, and the money stopped. She moved into a small apartment with her mother. It was farther from school — the only one they could afford and still remain inside the district.

She noticed her friends began to treat her differently. They didn't want to hang out with her as much, preferring Caitlyn, the new girl who spent money faster than Jordan ever imagined. And, as for the sales ladies at the stores? They eyed her suspiciously, like she was going to shoplift something. In fact, she didn't really have any friends left, except for Abby. Abby didn't have any money either, but she was popular because she played sports.

Jordan's mother could only give her a tiny allowance. Without money, shopping had no appeal, leaving Jordan with little to do to fill her time.

One day, as Jordan and Abby walked to class, Abby mentioned something about tryouts for the lacrosse team. Jordan never saw herself as an athlete, but with her old friends in scarce supply, she was willing to try anything. It would cost over a hundred dollars for all the fees and equipment to join the team. Jordan knew the money wouldn't come easily, if at all.

"Mom, I've been thinking about trying out for lacrosse at school."

"Oh, honey, I think that's a great idea. You know your father was a star athlete in high school. Maybe you have some of his talent."

"I don't know if I can make it, but I guess I can give it a try."

"When are tryouts?"

"Next week."

"Well, why don't you try for it? I'll bet you can do it."

"Mom, there's one other thing," Jordan hesitated. "If I make the team, I'll need about a hundred dollars."

Her mother sighed. "Jordan, I don't know if we can afford that. Doesn't the school have a way to pay for it?"

Jordan shook her head. "No, they cut the money for

that a couple of years ago."

Her mother looked away, not speaking for the longest time. She looked back at Jordan with tired eyes. "I don't know. I just don't know." Her voice trailed off.

Jordan decided to try out anyway. She had always believed if you wanted something badly enough, things would work out.

A week later she did try out, and to her surprise, she even made the team. She was so excited until her thoughts ran back to the money.

"Mom! Mom! Guess what?" She jumped up and down in her kitchen. "I made the team! I don't believe it."

Her mother beamed. "I'm so proud of you. I just knew you could do it."

"But Mom, I know we don't have the money. But it's okay. I just wanted to see if I could do it. The coach will understand. He's a cool guy."

Her mother got up and walked into the other room. Jordan heard her rummaging around in the closet. A minute later she returned. She was holding something in her hand. She reached out, placing Jordan's hand on top of hers. Jordan felt something like a piece of paper. Slowly, Jordan turned her hand over. There was a crisp, hundred-dollar bill in her palm. Her eyes flew open in surprise. It was a pittance compared to what she used to spend, but now it seemed like a fortune. She held her mother's gaze. Jordan knew the sacrifices her mother had to have made to find this money.

"Mom, are you sure we can . . .?"

Her mother smiled and nodded with tears in her eyes.

Life is certainly strange, thought Jordan, looking back on it now. She couldn't believe how her mother's love and that little bit of money could change her life so much.

She grabbed her lacrosse stick and rushed out the door.

* * *

Off the deep end: money attitude extremes

If you find yourself, like Jordan, buying things you don't need because you're bored, feel as though you need attention, or you just get a rush from buying them, then you likely spend more than you should. Extreme spenders often engage in *impulse buying*, or buying without thought, or *binge buying*, buying in a spree. On the other hand, if you find spending money makes you feel guilty, or you feel a sense of control, or power from having money, then you may miss out on some of the great opportunities in life. In extreme cases, heavy savers can become *misers* or *hoarders*.

Finding the proper balance is difficult. If it weren't, there wouldn't be so many people with out-of-control debts, or others who can't spend without intense feelings of guilt. While a proper balance is hard to achieve, and even harder to define, the extremes are easier to spot. Here's a short, two-part quiz designed to help you to understand your attitude toward spending and saving. You may find you have extreme tendencies that are unhealthy for you and your money.

Saver index quiz

1. I feel guilty when I spend money, even on necessities.

   never   sometimes   often   always

2. Money makes me feel in control.

   never   sometimes   often   always

3. I ask my friends for money, or to do things for me because it saves me money.

   never   sometimes   often   always

4. I find it impossible to spend money on others.

   never   sometimes   often   always

5. Having money makes me feel self-confident.

   never   sometimes   often   always

   Scoring:

For every question you answered with *never*, give yourself a 0. For every question you answered with *sometimes*, give yourself a 5. For every question you answered with *often*, give yourself a 10, and for *always* give yourself a 15.

Score	0 - 25:	*Weak Saver*
Score	30 - 45:	*Strong Saver*
Score	50 - 70:	*Extreme Saver*

Spender index quiz

1. I buy things I don't want or need.

   never   sometimes   often   always

2. I buy things when I'm bored.

   never   sometimes   often   always

3. I spend money to have a good time.

   never   sometimes   often   always

4. I believe that there will always be enough money for the things I want.

   never   sometimes   often   always

5. I buy things to impress my friends.

   never   sometimes   often   always

   Scoring:

For every question you answered with *never*, give yourself a 0. For every question you answered with *sometimes*, give yourself a 5. For every question you answered with *often*, give yourself a 10, and for *always* give yourself a 15.

Score	0 - 25:	*Weak Spender*
Score	30 - 45:	*Strong Spender*
Score	50 - 70:	*Extreme Spender*

You will most likely notice that a low score on the saver index means a high score on the spender index, and vice versa. On the other hand, you might have conflicting attitudes, which at times lead you to either over-spend or over-save, depending on the situation. This is normal. However, scores above 50 on either the saver or spender index indicate you have a tendency to save or spend too much.

If you have an extreme-spender score, your challenge will be to think about why you buy things. You will have to develop the discipline to turn your spending into a considered, conscious effort. Ask yourself the following questions before you spend money:

1. Do I need this or just want it? (See Chapter 1 for more on this.)
2. Do I have the money to pay for it without using credit?
3. Am I buying this because I'm bored or feeling down?
4. What else could I use the money for that would benefit my life more?
5. Have I shopped around and compared prices and features, or is this a spur-of-the-moment purchase?

If you have a very high saver score, your challenge will be to distinguish between buying those things that make life worth living, versus relying upon money to give you those feelings. Ask yourself these questions.

1. Do I frequently impose on my friends, such as bumming a ride or asking for a loan?
2. Can I feel good about a purchase after I have budgeted for it, knowing it has lasting value?
3. Does my need to save money result in poor

choices, like not replacing worn tires on my car?

4. Have I done anything recently for my parents or other special people in my life?

5. Will spending money now save me even more in the future, such as buying a magazine subscription rather than individual copies?

Borrowing is not evil

Your feelings about saving and spending may complicate your feelings toward borrowing; however, they shouldn't. Why? Because borrowing is a tool — one which you can use to help you to either spend or save.

Borrowing is not good, nor evil. It is a financial tool.

Your real money choices are to either spend or save. Period. Borrowing helps you to accomplish one or both of those choices. Think about it. You would never borrow just for the sake of borrowing. You borrow because you want to buy something, because you want to spend. But, you might also borrow to save money. Sound like a radical thought? Consider that you might borrow money to buy a television because it's on sale. Or you might borrow money to buy a house because mortgage payments are less than rent. Or you might borrow money to buy a car with lower maintenance and better fuel economy. In each of these instances, borrowing helps to both spend and save.

Again, borrowing is a tool. It is how you use this tool

that makes for either sound or poor money management.

Borrowing for the right reason is the foundation of smart money management.

In this chapter, we explored spending, saving, and borrowing. Some people are naturally inclined to spend and some to save, based upon their money personality and their money attitudes. Savers value money over the things it can buy, while spenders feel just the opposite. Extremes of each can be unhealthy for your money and yourself. Lastly, we looked at borrowing as a tool, which can be used to help you to spend, save, or both.

Terms covered in Chapter 6

- **Behavioral Finance**
- **Money Attitudes**
- **Impulse Buying**
- **Binge Buying**
- **Miser**
- **Hoarder**

Practical App: retailer tricks

Have you ever noticed that milk is located at the back of the grocery store? Or how about all of the candy bars and fan magazines located by the front register? Retailers place these items in these places as a way to influence your buying habits. When you have to hike to the back of the store to buy milk, you have to walk past a lot of other items you might purchase even if milk was all you really wanted. Items by the cash register are called impulse items because they are cheap and convenient to thoughtlessly throw into your shopping cart along with your other groceries.

You can resist these tactics by making a shopping list before you head to the store. Then, stick to it. Once again, if you make purchasing a conscious, rational effort, you will waste less money on those things you don't need.

7 Your Financial Statement

As you've probably guessed, sooner or later it would come to this: numbers, numbers, and more numbers. At some point, managing money means tracking the amount of dollars and cents you spend. So, as with dieting and exercise, it's something that takes a little effort to achieve results. That effort may, at times, be boring. However, the benefits substantially outweigh the efforts.

Managing your money is impossible without knowing what you've done with it.

A *financial statement* is a universally agreed-upon format to track the money you bring in and how you spend it. It's not really difficult to understand a financial statement; the math can be mastered by a fourth grader. The truly hard part is to do the required work to make one. It is a part of financial discipline that helps you manage your money to achieve your goals, be they a college education, a new car, or a new house.

There are lots of printed and electronic financial statement forms, but they are all based on the format presented in this chapter. Regardless of the form you use, you still have to do the work. Sometimes life is that way — you have to memorize the multiplication tables and the state capitals. That's just the way it is.

So, what exactly is a financial statement?

A financial statement is a powerful financial tool that tells you what you've done with your money in the past as a way to help you plan for the future.

Managing your money without a financial statement is like shopping online without access to your shopping cart. Without it, you'd have to remember everything you placed in your cart from memory. Did I buy one of those or two? I found another one on sale; how much did I pay for the first one? Have I spent enough to qualify for free shipping? Remembering these details may not be difficult to accomplish with a handful of items, but what about twenty, thirty, or even fifty? The same thing applies to your monthly expenses. You may think you can remember all of the details, but it's unlikely.

A financial statement tracks all of the money you brought in during the month in one section and all of the money you spent in another. Your *bottom line,* or the difference between the two, is the money you have left over to spend next month; or if you overspend, it's the money you need to withdraw from savings or borrow to cover the shortfall. It's that simple.

A financial statement shows how much money you brought in versus how much you spent. Your bottom line is the difference between the two.

Most often, financial statements are broken into monthly chunks because most expenses are paid monthly: cell phones, utilities, membership fees, cable

TV, etc. It is also helpful to group expenses together in categories, such as car expenses for gas, oil, and repairs; or entertainment expenses for concert tickets, sodas, and lunches.

At the end of each month, everything you have spent money for, including any debt payments, are totaled. Likewise, all of the money you earned or were given, as in an allowance, is totaled. If you earned more than you spent, then you have extra money. If you spent more than you earned, then you have to borrow or take some out of savings.

Financial statements can be simple or complex, depending upon the level of detail with which you want to track your money. However, a simple financial statement is better than none. And, a simple financial statement takes less effort, so you are more likely to do the necessary work to maintain it.

It begins with a financial statement

Exhibit 7.1 is an example of a simple, three-month financial statement. Notice that the months run in columns from left to right, while the various income and expense items related to each month are shown in rows. Typically, income items are shown in the uppermost rows with the expenses shown below them. This is the way accountants prepare financial statements, and it is the accepted format for banks and other lenders.

This is called a *cashflow* statement because it simply records when money is spent or received. It makes no attempt to adjust for timing differences between when you pay for something and when you receive the benefit. Car insurance is a good example. You pay a premium up front, but you receive coverage over the ensuing six months. In actuality, you are spending one sixth of the premium every month. This concept of matching expenses and income is called *accrual* accounting. It is a more sophisticated way to manage money. However, for our purposes, a cashflow budget will suffice.

The last line at the bottom of each monthly column is aptly called the bottom line, which is the total of the expense items subtracted from the total of the income items. If income exceeded expenses, then there is a positive bottom line; more money is left at the end of the month than at the beginning. Conversely, if expenses exceeded income, then there is a negative bottom line, shown in ( ); there is less money at month end than at the start.

The far right column shows the total for each income and expense item for all three months. This total is helpful as it gives a better picture of your finances over time. Some income and expense items can vary quite a bit from month to month, requiring several months to see a pattern. For example, you may not incur the expense for car repairs every month, but you might incur them regularly in any three or six-month period.

This is the value of a financial statement containing multiple months of data

Exhibit 7.1 Cashflow Financial Statement

Income $	June	July	Aug	Total
Allowance	200	200	200	600
Job	310	300	350	960
Gifts	100	0	50	150
Total $	610	500	600	1,710
Expenses $				
Cell Phone	100	90	80	270
Sports Fees	15	50	0	65
Clothes	200	300	400	900
Entertainment	50	45	30	125
Car	50	150	40	240
Credit Card	25	25	25	75
Total $	440	660	575	1675
Bottom Line $	170	(160)	25	35

Here's a trick accountants use: the bottom line of the last column has to equal the total of the bottom lines for June, July, and August. This is a double check on the accuracy of the addition for the entire financial statement. If there is a bad entry, or the math is incorrect, then the two totals won't match up.

Now, here are some questions to help you understand how to use the information contained in Exhibit 7.1.

1. In which month did expenses exceed income?
2. Are clothing expenses increasing or decreasing?
3. What month would show a negative bottom line if there was no gift income?
4. What might have happened in July that caused the car expenses to dramatically increase?
5. At the end of three months, was there money left over or not? Answers.
   1. July
   2. Increasing
   3. August
   4. Car repairs
   5. Left over

Did you get all that? Whew, so many numbers.

Stay positive: your net worth

You'll soon discover how useful a financial statement can be. However, before we explore that, we need to add another detail. While the financial statement in Exhibit 7.1 tracks income and expenses, we also need to see what happened to savings, checking, and borrowing for the same period of time.

Whenever the bottom line is negative, you have to either use money from savings and checking, or you have to borrow it to make up for the loss. Those are the only possibilities (not counting a gift of money, which is nice to have, but not predictable). So, we need to track the amount of savings, checking, and debt at the beginning of the financial statement and then compare it to the end to see if our financial resources (savings or borrowing capacity) are increasing or decreasing. First, there are some new terms you will need to know. In accounting lingo, money in your checking and savings accounts is called *assets*. Loans, such as credit card debt and car loans, are called *liabilities*. Subtracting the liabilities from the assets yields a number referred to as *net worth*. If assets are greater than liabilities, then net worth is positive. If liabilities are greater than assets, then net worth is negative.

The ultimate goal of money management is to increase positive net worth.

The greater your positive net worth, meaning you have more assets than liabilities, the more financial resources you have to meet your financial goals.

Banks and lenders will seldom, if ever, lend to individuals with a negative net worth. Why? Because those individuals have no resources to handle a financial setback, like a large, unexpected bill for car repairs or medical expenses. And banks don't like that.

If you want to get a loan or other credit, you will need a positive net worth.

The ultimate balancing act: your balance sheet

Exhibit 7.2 compares the change in net worth accompanying the cashflow statement in Exhibit 7.1. This comparison statement is called a balance sheet because the assets equal, or balance, the liabilities plus net worth.

Exhibit 7.2 Balance Sheet

Assets $	June Beg.	Aug End
Savings	500	530
Checking	50	50
Total $	550	580
Liabilities $		
Credit Card Balance	500	425
Total $	500	425
Net Worth $	50	155

You'll first notice that net worth is both positive at the beginning and the end. It also increased by $105 — a good thing. Why did this happen? Because assets increased and liabilities decreased. If you go back to the *Exhibit 7.1* Financial Statement, you can see that the bottom line increased by $30 over the three-month period. That's $30 more money added to savings in *Exhibit 7.2*. The real improvement, however, came from reducing liabilities. In *Exhibit 7.1*, there were three credit card payments, which in total reduced the credit card debt by $75. As you can see in *Exhibit 7.2,* the liabilities were reduced by the same $75.

Hopefully, you will begin to see how the financial statement from *Exhibit 7.1* relates to balance sheet in *Exhibit 7.2.* If your bottom line is negative, meaning you spent more than you made, then net worth also decreases. Why? Because you have to withdraw money from savings, decreasing your assets. Alternatively, you may have to borrow money, increasing your liabilities and lowering your net worth.

You can think of net worth like a reservoir of money resources and your financial statement like two streams. A positive bottom line from your financial statement is a stream that fills the reservoir, increasing your financial resources. A negative bottom line from your financial statement is another stream that drains the reservoir, decreasing your financial resources.

Monthly income, expenses, and borrowing all directly affect your net worth.

You should also note in the earlier example, net worth can be increased by either increasing assets or reducing liabilities. This is a powerful concept that provides many options to manage your net worth. Don't worry if this all seems confusing right now. These are advanced concepts which only begin to make more sense as you work with your own financial and balance sheet statements.

So, what have we learned at this point? A cashflow statement records income and expenses for some time period. Subtracting expenses from income yields a bottom line. If the bottom line is positive, then checking or savings — also called assets — will increase as well. If the bottom line is negative, then either savings must be decreased or debt — also called liabilities — must be increased to cover the overspending.

The result of subtracting liabilities from assets is called net worth. It is the bottom line of a balance sheet. If liabilities exceed assets, net worth is negative. If assets exceed liabilities, net worth is positive. A positive net worth is the financial resource you can use to meet your future financial needs. A negative net worth means you have no financial resources to meet your financial needs.

Where's the plug? cash leakage

There is one practical detail concerning financial statements that you should bear in mind. Money that goes into your wallet is hard to track. It is called *cash leakage.*

Cash leakage is the cash you spend from your pocket or wallet. As a result, you have few or no records to track how it was spent.

There are usually no invoices to refer to in order to see how much you spent and on what you spent. One way to keep track is to set a limit on the amount of cash you use, like ten dollars a week. Then you need only note cash expenditures as a single category in your financial statement, without the need for more detail. Use a credit card to pay for any other, larger expenses. Just don't forget to pay off the balance before the grace period expires. Try to get into the habit of thinking about credit card purchases as if they were the same as using cash out of your pocket. If you know you have to completely pay them off at the end of the month, you won't be tempted to borrow instead.

There are many ready-made financial statement worksheets, both printed and in electronic form. Alternately, you can use a spreadsheet program, like Microsoft Excel, by following the format shown in *Exhibit 7.1*. You will want to include twelve months instead of only three. It's not important what type of worksheet you use to create your financial statement, so long as it contains enough detail to be useful. How much is enough detail? Generally, a large income or expense item that includes a number of components requires more detailed tracking. For example, a large entertainment expense might need to be further broken down into travel, meals, concert tickets, and other events. A category with large, monthly swings may also need to be broken down to better understand what is happening.

In the next chapter, we'll cover the many ways you can use your financial statement to better manage your money and achieve your goals.

Terms covered in Chapter 7

- **Financial Statement**
- **Cashflow**
- **Accrual**
- **Bottom Line**
- **Assets**
- **Liabilities**
- **Net Worth**
- **Cash Leakage**

Practical App: first steps

A good way to get started making your financial statement is to keep every receipt from everything you purchase for two months. Place these into an envelope, one envelope for each month. Now, record every one of these receipts in your financial statement using either the format from this chapter or a prepared form. From this snapshot, you may be surprised by what you discover.

If you do nothing else, look at the areas where you are spending the most money and track those as a priority. It may be for clothes, iTunes, gas for your car, or video games. Once you see how you actually spend your money, you can begin planning to improve your money choices.

8   Budgeting Savvy

It seemed as though every month outlasted Aiden's money. Try as he might, he just couldn't come out ahead. There was always some unpleasant surprise: a large cell phone bill, the snacks for that party at his friend's house, and as always, those credit card payments.

And when he came up short, his only alternative was to borrow more. As a result, his credit card debt kept increasing as well; it was over $800 and steadily growing. Fortunately, he hadn't missed any payments, but he certainly wasn't making any progress toward paying his debt down either.

The worst part of it was that he couldn't remember where all his money went. Of course, he knew keeping his car on the road cost a lot, but he had no choice about paying for those costs. Without a car, he couldn't get to his job or to the sporting events at school.

And, he just had to use his cell phone, despite those awful overages. After all, his friends knew him as the "go to" guy.

Then, there were the iTunes. How could he get through the day without his music? What happened to the rest of his money? He really didn't have a clue.

Aiden had a full schedule; he'd taken on advanced placement classes, on top of baseball practice, on top of several clubs he'd joined to polish his college application. As if that wasn't enough, he worked weekends at a local tourist attraction doing odd jobs and helping the owner, Mr. Kuan, run the concession stand.

Aiden liked Mr. Kuan, a middle-aged man who always had a smile for everyone and always seemed so in control. There were never any emergencies or crises at work. Mr. Kuan keep things running smoothly, even when there were setbacks, like the time the city closed off the street in front of his entry gate for a week so that they could repair the pavement. Mr. Kuan took it all in stride. He even managed to keep everyone on the payroll, confident that it would all work out.

One afternoon, when things were a little quiet at the concession stand, Aiden got into a conversation with Mr. Kuan about finances.

"Mr. Kuan, can I ask you something about managing money?" asked Aiden.

"What's on your mind?"

"Well, I just can't seem to get ahead. Even when I work more hours, the money just seems to vanish. I try to set some aside, but there's always something that comes up every month. Then, I end up in a deeper hole." Aiden shook his head.

Mr. Kuan smiled. "You know, when I first started this business, I had the same problem. There were a lot of times I just didn't know where I'd get enough money to pay everyone, let alone pay myself."

"So what'd you do?"

"It was very hard at first. I didn't know what to do. But I knew I couldn't keep living like that. So I thought about it . . . a lot. Finally I hit on an idea." Mr. Kuan pointed toward his office, motioning with a nod for Aiden to follow. They stepped inside, and Mr. Kuan pointed at five coffee cans lined up on a shelf behind his desk.

"Do you see those cans?" asked Mr. Kuan.

Aiden nodded.

"Each can used to have a label on it. Over the years, they have all fallen off. But, I still know what each one is for," said Mr. Kuan, beaming with pride. "The first can I labeled *elephant*. In it, I put every bill that I have to pay no matter what. If I don't pay for those things in the *elephant*, I have no business: bills for my mortgage, utilities, and things like that.

"The next can, I labeled the *trainer*. In that one, I put every bill that feeds the elephant, keeps the elephant healthy. Like keeping the heat on in the winter and making repairs around here."

Mr. Kuan squinted at Aiden to see if he was still listening. Aiden nodded as he tried to understand.

"The third can, I labeled the *tent*. It's for those things that make this place attractive and interesting, that draw attention. Things like advertising and fresh paint on the buildings."

Aiden stared at the cans, fascinated by Mr. Kuan's strange system.

"The fourth can, I labeled the *reins* for those bills that keep my business on track for the future. If a person used my system, the *reins* might be something like college. For my business, it's training for my employees and upgrading our facilities."

Mr. Kuan turned to walk away.

Aiden stared after him, uncertain what to do next. Finally, Aiden stammered, "What's the last can for?"

Mr. Kuan walked back over to it. He flipped it upside down and then shook it in the air. It was empty. "This one, I labeled *manure,* for the bills from everything else. I don't like to clean up any more manure than I have to, so I make sure I don't fill it up in the first place." Mr. Kuan laughed at Aiden's expression and walked to the front to wait on a customer.

Aiden stared at the *manure* can. He wondered just how many of his bills belonged in that can.

Your ticket to the future: your budget

How many of your expenses belong in the manure can? If you don't keep track, you'll never know. And once you do, you may be surprised at what you learn. But that's only part of the process. The other part is to do something about it. You have to make an effort to keep the manure can empty. That's what budgeting is all about.

You've probably heard about budgeting. And, while you may not know exactly what it is, you probably know you want no part of it. Budgeting often gets a bad rap. In fact, here's what some others have had to say about it.

> "It's clearly a budget. It's got a lot of numbers in it."
>
> George Bush, 43rd U.S. President

> "A budget tells us what we can't afford, but it doesn't keep us from buying it."
>
> William Feather

> "A budget is telling your money where to go instead of wondering where it went."
>
> Dave Ramsey

> "A budget is just a method of worrying before you spend money, as well as afterward."
>
> Unknown

You'll soon find, though, a budget is another tool you can use to turn your dreams into reality. You may be surprised to learn that you already know what a budget is. Here's a hint: it looks the same as a financial statement.

A budget is a financial statement showing how you plan to use your money in the future.

A financial statement looks at the past—what happened to your money — while a budget is a financial statement that looks toward the future — what you plan to do with your money. That's easy. A budget uses the same format as a financial statement.

The first step in making a budget, therefore, is to begin with the blank financial statement format. The months still run along the top (usually twelve months) and the same income and expense items will run down the left side. You will fill in the rest of it based upon the information from your financial statement.

How do you use your financial statement as a guide to building a budget? Your financial statement tells you which things you can change and which will likely stay the same in the future. Things like car loan payments and cable TV bills will probably stay the same. Did you consistently overspend on other items, like entertainment or your cell phone? Maybe you can change these. What about credit card payments? Or clothes expenses? After preparing a financial statement, many people are surprised to learn they spent a lot more than they thought on things that didn't amount to much.

Armed with the information from your financial statement, you can begin to fill in the numbers in your budget. Start by filling in all of the items that will stay the same. Then, fill in the others you know will change, such as expiring magazine subscriptions or one-time athletic fees. Finally, you can begin to fill in the amounts for those things you plan to change because you are making a conscious choice to control them, like cutting back on apps or working more hours at a part-time job. The choice is yours.

A budget provides a way to look at a lot of little changes, which, in total, help you meet your money goals. It is a chance for you to decide to spend your money in a more conscious and intelligent way. You may want to save money for a big purchase like a car, house, college education, or even give more of it to charity.

It's all a question of priorities — of setting goals. You use a budget as a way to make better use of your money. For example, after studying your financial statement, you may find you spend an average of $5 per weekday at Starbucks. Over the course of a month, that adds up to $150. Hmm. That's a fair amount of change. Maybe, you think, if I could cut that spending to $2.50 per day, in a year's time I would have saved $650. What could I do with an extra $650? In your budget, you can plan how to make the best use of that extra money.

It's your choice: budgeting priorities

And what are the best priorities to choose for your budget? How do you decide on the best financial goals? The answers are as diverse as every one of you reading this book. Everyone has a dream, the majority of which are powered by money. However, there are a few, simple, initial goals with which most financial planners agree. These have been proven time and again to be wise first steps for anyone who wants to build a solid financial foundation for the rest of their lives.

Priority 1: start an emergency fund

Life is unpredictable: cars break, phones get lost, prices go up. If you don't have extra money, every unexpected event escalates from an irritation to a crisis. You can't depend, nor do you want to depend, upon borrowing your way out of future money troubles. That only sets you up for a bigger crisis the next time around. This is so obvious it is often overlooked. Hoping everything will turn out okay is not a plan; it is a denial of reality. An emergency fund is like shock absorbers on a car. Without them, your ride will be very bumpy.

Start with a savings account with the aim to build it up to at least the equivalent of six months' worth of spending. How much is six months of spending? Look at your financial statement. What could you reduce or eliminate to accumulate six months' worth of savings? Look at your financial statement. Are your credit card payments preventing you from adding to your savings? Look at your financial statement. You get the idea.

Now you can begin to see how a financial statement and a budget work together. Knowing what you did with your money in the past forms the basis for what you intend to do with it in the future.

If you use an electronic spreadsheet, you can test out different combinations of spending and saving strategies. This is one benefit of using an electronic budgeting format. Assessing the total impact from a lot of small changes is almost impossible to do in your head.

One warning, though — be realistic. Don't create spending goals you can't live up to. If you spend forty dollars a month on your cell phone and that's the minimum plan, then you can't budget for anything less.

Priority 2: pay down debt

The next priority is to better manage your debt. If you are only making minimum credit card payments, as discussed in a previous chapter, you might never pay off the balance. That is money you could use to achieve your goals, instead.

If you fail to use your money to achieve your goals, others will use it to achieve theirs.

A sad but true statement. You can be sure that businesses of every kind spare no effort to get more of your money to reach their goals: premium channels on cable TV, new video games, unlimited texting, and faster Internet. These have all been created by businesses to entice you to spend more of your money so that they can reach their goals.

Even worse, when people run out of their own money, they borrow even more of it. Think about it. People are going into debt to spend even more money to help others reach their goals.

How do you turn this around? Look at your financial statement. How much are you spending on credit card payments? On a car loan? There is a generally accepted benchmark, or "rule of thumb," lenders use to decide if you have too much debt. This is a maximum limit and one you should ideally never even come close to. However, when you first start out in life, you may occasionally bump up against this limit.

This debt benchmark is expressed as a ratio. A *ratio* is a way to compare one number to another. Huh? What's that mean? Don't panic, you use ratios all the time. Two-thirds of a cup of flour is a ratio. If you divide a cup into thirds, the correct amount of flour will take up two of those thirds. How about test scores? You got a ninety. Doesn't mean much until you know there was a total possible score of one hundred. What if you found out that the total possible score was a thousand? That ninety doesn't look so good now.

A *debt ratio* is measured the same way. It is the ratio of the total amount of money you spend on monthly loan payments as compared with the total amount of money you bring in for the month. (The debt portion of the ratio is based on the total of your *payments*, not the total amount of your *debt*.)

What is considered a reasonable debt ratio? The FHA, or Federal Housing Authority, which insures millions of loans to homeowners, suggests 43 percent as a maximum. For example, if you bring in $1,000 in a month and spend $430 on your loan payments, you have a debt ratio of $430 divided $1,000 = 43%.

There are a number of details you should bear in mind when you calculate this ratio. First, your income does not include money you receive from allowances and gifts. Lenders feel this money cannot be depended upon in the future. Secondly, any income from your job should be the gross amount you earn, before taxes are subtracted.

Thirdly, the debt payment part of the ratio is the sum of the minimum required payments for all of the following: auto loans, student loans, personal loans, and credit cards.

Finally, payments for utility bills, car insurance, health insurance, and cell phones do not count. If you have a mortgage, you need to include your principal and interest, plus taxes and insurance as part of the payment.

If your debt ratio is anywhere near 43 percent, one of your budget priorities should be to pay down your debt. Even if your debt payments are much lower than the maximum, you still should consider paying down your debt. Why? Because some day you may want to borrow money for a car or a house, and your existing debt will count against you. In other words, it will limit your *debt capacity*, or future ability to borrow money.

At last, we get to the fun part of budgeting. Fun? How could budgeting ever be fun?

Priority 3: pay yourself first

What's your dream? A car? A college education? A new home? An exotic vacation? A budget is your ticket to make it happen. Now you know where to find that money, and with your budget you can decide how to take control of it.

One way to pay yourself first is to put money into savings before you make any other payments. Try to make savings contributions as fixed in your mind as car payments. Pretty soon, it will become a habit.

Using your budget, you can plan to reduce your debt payments, eliminate thoughtless spending, and save money for those things that can truly change your life. Wouldn't you trade fewer iTunes, shoes, and concert tickets for a car? You decide. Your budget can provide the road map.

Reality check: budget versus actual

There is one final step. Every month, or maybe every three months, you should create a new financial statement and then compare it with your budget for the same period of time. Did you stay on track? Did you reduce your debt as you planned? Did you keep your spending under control? If you didn't meet your budget numbers, then you need to consider making a new budget with more realistic numbers, or maybe you need to try harder. Either way, don't give up. Getting it right is worth the effort.

Failing to compare your plans with what actually happened is like driving a car without looking up from your map.

You may have a great route picked out, but you're never

going to get there. The process is pretty simple. Make a budget, compare it with your financial statement, revise the budget, and then compare it with the next financial statement, and so on.

There are several web sites that you can use to streamline the budgeting process. One is Mint.com which claims to have over seven million users and has won awards from respected financial planning organizations.

In this chapter, we looked at how you use your financial statement to prepare a budget. A budget is a plan to achieve your financial priorities. Sound financial management calls for three initial goals: first, build an emergency fund; second, pay down debt; and third, pay yourself first. Then, periodically compare your actual financial statement with your budget. Make appropriate changes to stay on track.

Terms covered in Chapter 8

- **Emergency Fund**
- **Budget**
- **Debt Ratio**
- **Debt Capacity**

Practical App: starting your budget

How do you begin budgeting? First, decide on a simple goal. Make it one that you can achieve in a short period of time, say three months. It could be as simple as saving $100, or paying down a credit card balance, or paying cash for a new pair of running shoes. Next, look over your financial statement and then decide what items you can reduce, or eliminate for three months to achieve your goal. You might be able to reduce the number of iTunes you order or cut out a few lunches. It doesn't matter as long as, in total, the changes in your spending add up to meet your goal.

Now, write down the amount you intend to spend on each of those items. Check monthly to see if you are staying on track. If you get off track the first month, try to get back on track the next month. At the end of three months, check to see if you've accomplished your goal. If you did, congratulate yourself. If you didn't, make another goal and try again. Remember, you are practicing a new behavior. It may take some time to get it right. This is a skill you will use the rest of your life.

9 Checking Account Savvy

In previous chapters, you learned about some of the more common financial products and services provided by banks, including checking accounts, saving accounts, debit cards, and credit cards. In this chapter, you will gain a deeper understanding of checking accounts — how they work and how to manage them. Take the time to understand this material. It is the foundation upon which all of the newer, electronic services are based.

Within the last ten years, there has been an explosion in the variety and use of electronic funds transfer. Banks continue to dream up more and more ways for their customers to access their money anywhere and at any time of their choosing. However, all of these new products and services are based upon the mechanics of the humble, paper-based checking account.

Paper checks didn't die out with the dinosaurs

Let's say your Uncle Basil gives you a check for $100. You take it down to your bank and deposit it into your account. Up until 2004, that check had to physically travel by truck or airplane back to your uncle's bank where it would be *cleared*, provided your uncle had enough money in his account to cover it. If he didn't, then the check would be stamped *NSF*, meaning "not sufficient funds" and "bounced" back to your bank. All of this was both messy and time consuming. In 2004, a new federal law, *Check 21,* allowed banks to substitute digital check images for the actual checks. This innovation allowed banks to move checks electronically, greatly speeding up the processing of paper checks.

With electronic banking, a whole new range of services came into being. Most recently, smart phones, like the Apple iPhone, now provide customers with twenty-four hour access to their accounts. To someone who is struggling to understand basic banking accounts, like checking and savings, these new products and services may seem overwhelming. And, there is a temptation to assume that the newer services are just like the old ones. This, however, is not the case. While they are similar, there are important differences which you should understand when you use them.

The inside scoop: how banks work

Before we jump into all of that, you might have a very basic question, like: what is a bank? The simple answer is that a bank is a business. It doesn't make things, like computers or skateboards, or even sell things, like a grocery store. Mainly banks make money by lending it out. And where do they get the money to lend? They get some of it from you, me, and many others who put their money into savings and checking accounts. The bank lends that money out at a high interest rate, pays a lower rate for the accounts the money came from, and keeps the difference.

Consider this example: you deposit $1,000 into savings and the bank pays you 2 percent interest. In a year's time, you will make $20, i.e. $1,000 x .02 = $20. That's what the bank pays you for your savings. Now, let's say during that same year, the bank lends that same $1,000 out at 12 percent to a customer who borrows money on her credit card. The bank charges that customer $120, i.e. $1,000.00 x .12 = $120 for the credit card loan. The difference between the $20 the bank pays you and the $120 the bank charges the customer, in this case $100, is money the bank gets to keep.

The bank uses this money to cover the costs of its employees and facilities and to provide for a profit. Sounds like a pretty good deal for the bank, right? However, what happens when one customer fails to pay back his or her loan? In the above example, not only does the bank not get the $120 in interest, it must also use $1,000 of its own money to deposit into your savings account so you aren't out anything. As you can see, one bad loan wipes out all of the income the bank earned from more than nine other customers. Still think banking is a good business?

The shirt off of your back: what is a check?

You're probably familiar with paper checks. You may have even used them if you have a checking account. But what makes a valid check?

Exhibit 9.1 A Paper Check

A check is a written set of instructions telling the bank to transfer a specific amount of funds to another individual or organization.

Exhibit 9.1 is a picture of a typical personal check. Every valid check has the same elements: the account owner's name, the date, the words "pay to the order of" followed by the *payee's* name (the person or organization you intend to pay), the dollar amount both in numerical and written form, the name and location of the bank where the account is held, and the signature of the account owner. There are no other requirements as to size, shape, or even that it be written on paper. It could, for instance, be written on a T-shirt. As long as the above elements are included, it would be a valid check. The numbers at the bottom are printed in a very specific location and use magnetic ink. Together, these features make automatic processing possible. Starting on the far right, the routing number (the electronic address of the bank) is printed first followed by the checking account number and then the check number.

When you receive a check and want to deposit it, you, as the payee, must sign it on the back, called an *endorsement*. You must sign in a predetermined place near one end, which once again speeds up processing. Once a check is endorsed and the money is withdrawn from the checking account of whoever wrote it, their bank then marks the reverse side, or cancels the check, preventing its reuse.

Banks have specific standards for check sizes, background colors, paper weight, and other requirements. Again, none of these are requirements for a valid check, but failing to use a standard check format will result in processing delays and potential confusion.

The paper trail: check register

Now that you know what makes a valid check, let's look at how to keep track of your checks. Most checks come packaged in batches of around thirty checks along with a form called a check register as shown below.

Exhibit 9.2 Check Register

CheckNum	Date	Description	Amount	Fee	Deposit	Balance
	8/10	Deposit			100.00	100.00
101	8/12	Tunes	20.00			80.00
102	8/15	Super Sports	35.00			45.00
	8/20	Cash - Deposit			20.00	65.00
103	8/22	Joe's - dinner	25.00			40.00
	8/21	Check acct fee		12.00		28.00
104	8/25	Coffee	5.00			23.00

A check register is a handy place to record key information about the checks you have written as well as the remaining amount of money you have to pay for them.

Starting on the far left in *Exhibit 9.2*, you begin by recording the check number, date, and payee for each check you write. In the column headed *Amount* you record the dollar amount of the check.

Similarly, when you make a deposit, you record it on a separate line and fill in the amount under the column headed *deposit*. You need record only the date of the deposit and the amount.

When you first start a checking account, you begin with a deposit, for which you record the date of the deposit and the amount. Next to that, in the last column headed *Balance*, you also record that same amount. This is the amount of money you have to cover future checks. After you write your first check, you record the appropriate information on the next line down in the register. You must now subtract the amount of that check from the balance, leaving you with a new balance, which you record in the column headed *Balance*. This is now the money you have left to spend. For the next check, you again record the information on the next line down and again subtract that amount from the balance and so on until you reach a balance of zero, in which case you have no more money. You should stop writing checks at his point.

When your checking account balance reaches zero, stop writing checks.

You then need to make a deposit to refill your account. You record the deposit in the check register on a separate line, again filling in only the date and amount. As before, this amount is also added to the previous balance in the column headed *Balance*.

Say it ain't so: checking fees

Finally, there is a column entitled "Fee." Here you record other deductions from your checking account that do not result from writing a check. Most often this will be fees for such things as the monthly maintenance cost for your checking account or an *overdraft fee,* which is a fee the bank charges should you accidentally write a check for more money than you have in your account.

In Chapter 1, we covered retailer tactics relating to fees and anchoring. As you will recall, one price for an extensive package of goods and services is used as an anchor, or yardstick, against which fees for related items are compared. These related items, which were originally included in the larger bundle, or package, are now priced separately. Because psychologically you are anchored on the larger, package price, the smaller fees for these related items are either ignored or viewed as relatively inexpensive.

Here's how it works for banking services. Let's say the

true cost to a bank of providing a checking account is $20 per month. The bank knows that most customers will shop around for a checking account with the lowest monthly maintenance expense, partly because they heavily promote and advertise this information. However, the bank still has to make up for any shortfall from the $20 a month. They accomplish this by charging fees for various checking-account-related services. An almost universal fee is the charge banks levy for overdrafts, or checks which lack sufficient funds to cover them. The fees that banks charge for these overdrafts range anywhere from $25 to $35 or more per occurrence. The bank is betting that its customers will write enough overdrafts, along with other items for which they charge fees, to make up for the lower, advertised monthly maintenance fee.

Fees can also be collected in other ways; some of which are not as obvious. For example, banks may require checking account customers to keep a minimum balance in their accounts. As long as the balance never falls below a set amount, such as $1,500, checking account maintenance fees are waived. Should the balance fall below that amount, even briefly, the bank will charge the full monthly fee.

You need only recall our earlier discussion about how a bank makes money to see how a minimum balance can constitute a fee. These checking account balances provide money that the bank can lend out to earn interest income. The bank is, once again, betting that it can make more money lending this money out than by charging account holders the true, monthly maintenance fee.

Some banks have become even more creative in how they charge for unbundled, checking-related services. At the end of each month, banks typically mail out an accounting of the checks you have written over the previous month. You might call this the bank's check register, and we'll look at how it relates to the one you keep in a moment. Typically, the bank's check register, or *checking account statement*, includes a photocopy of all of the checks it has received from the individuals and organizations who have cashed your checks for that month. Although most banks include this expense in the monthly maintenance fee, some banks now charge for photocopies of checks.

Yet another tactic is to charge for printed statements sent through the mail as opposed to digital copies made available online. Prior to the Internet, the US mail was the only option banks had to contact their customers. They really had no choice but to include this in their checking account bundle, a choice which some banks now feel they can force upon their customers and charge them accordingly.

Stick'em up: check forgery

One of the reasons you will want to review your bank statement and copies of your *canceled* checks is to make sure that someone, other than yourself, hasn't written a check on your account. *Forgeries,* or fake checks, are checks made to look like you wrote them, including an illegitimate copy of your signature. You have to safeguard your checking account from forgers by monitoring your canceled checks. There are strict time limits as to how long you can wait to report forgeries and get your money back from the bank.

Just do it: balancing your checking account

After you receive your monthly bank statement, you should compare the final checking account balance to the one in your personal check register. This process is called *"balancing your checking account."* Often the bank statement balance will not match your personal balance. Why? Because the bank may not know about all of the checks you have written since the statement was mailed. That check you wrote to Cousin Griffin may end up in a desk drawer for a month because he forgot about it. You have it recorded in your check register, but the bank knows nothing about it.

To keep things simple, we'll consider only paper checks for now, ignoring debit cards and other electronic checking (covered in a later chapter). Here is how you balance your checkbook, or in other words, match up your personal check register with your bank statement.

How to balance your checkbook

Step 1. On a separate sheet of paper, write down the ending balance from the bank statement.

Step 2. Match your personal check register with the bank statement and determine which checks you have written that the bank has not included. Hint: if you write checks in numerical order, any missing checks from the bank statement will be apparent. Total the amount of these checks and subtract that amount from the bank statement balance in Step 1.

Step 3. Now match the deposits you show in your check register with the bank statement and determine which deposits the bank has not recorded. Total these and add that number to the balance from Step 2.

Step 4. Add up any fees shown in the bank statement you haven't recorded in your check register and subtract this total from the result in Step 3. If there are any fees shown that are incorrect or you don't understand, make a note of these, but still include them in your adjustment. You will want to talk with your bank later to either understand them or dispute them.

The resulting balance you calculated in Step 4 should match the balance in your checkbook register.

If it doesn't, you will have to do a little more research to find out why it doesn't. It may be your math is wrong or the bank may have made a mistake.

The first reason you want to balance your checkbook is to catch mistakes made by the bank, which can happen, particularly in light of the many fees they now charge. Secondly, there are time limits imposed by the bank and federal laws limiting how long you have to report these mistakes, so the sooner you are aware of them, the better.

As mentioned above, bank fraud, including everything from check forgery to unauthorized debit card usage, has become a commonplace event. Under the Fair Credit Billing Act, you have up to 60 days from the date of your bank statement to notify your bank to prevent any loss of money. (Beware, this notification has to be in writing to fully protect your rights.)

Thirdly, you may have made a mistake in your check register. If you don't catch it, you might end up inadvertently overdrawing your account, costing you money and possibly hurting your credit score. The sooner you catch a mistake, the less you will have to dig through to find it.

In this chapter, we covered the basic checking account with an emphasis on paper checks. You learned what makes a valid check and what happens to a check after you write it. Keeping track of your checks and reconciling your check register with the monthly bank statement is a way to catch errors before you lose the opportunity to recover your losses under current credit laws. Fees have become an everyday reality of banking. Understanding fees and keeping them to a minimum is the way you keep more of your money working for you.

In the next chapter, we will build on your knowledge of paper-based checking as we delve into the newer, electronic banking products.

Terms covered in Chapter 9

- **Cleared Check**
- **NSF**
- **Payee**
- **Endorsement**
- **Canceled Check**
- **Check Register**
- **Bank Statement**
- **Forgery**
- **Balance**
- **Bundle**
- **Overdraft**
- **Reconcile**

Practical App: your check register

Make it a habit to record every deposit and check in your check register. Fill out all of the information it requires. Then compare that with your bank statement at the end of the month.

You may want to put off balancing your checkbook until you have read the next chapter about debit cards as their charges will also be included in your bank statement. At that point, you will have all the information you need to balance your checking account.

For now, you should just note some of the following information. Which checks are not included in the bank statement that you have written? Which of your deposits do not show up in the bank statement? Look at any bank fees. Do you understand all of them?

10   Electronic Banking

In the last chapter, you learned about paper-based checking accounts. In today's world, most banking services are done electronically. However, the same basic concepts, discussed previously, still apply. Whether you use paper checks or electronic banking, you still need money in your account to cover withdrawals.

Fast, fast, fast: electronic funds transfer

One of the major differences between traditional banking and electronic banking is that things happen a lot faster with electronic banking. *Electronic Funds Transfer, or EFT,* is the name applied to this wide range of electronic banking services. This fast pace can be a good thing, but it can also be a bad thing if you don't understand your rights and responsibilities when you use them.

First the simple things: credit and debit cards

Let's begin with two very common forms of electronic banking: debit and credit cards. When you use one of these cards to pay for a purchase, you typically swipe the card through a card reader, sending certain information about your bank account, along with the purchase information, through an electronic network that eventually reaches your bank. You authorize the use of credit card payments with your signature, and for debit cards you use a *PIN* or Personal Identification Number. This is a four digit number selected by you, which you must safeguard to prevent others from using your card without your permission.

Hint: when you select a PIN, try not to use easily guessed numbers from your birth date, street address, or zip code. Avoid writing it down if you can. If you must write it down, keep it separate from your wallet and your card.

While credit cards and debit cards both allow you to make a purchase, they work in entirely different ways. They are even subject to different federal laws.

Debit cards use money from your checking account. Credit cards use money loaned to you by the bank or other credit card issuer.

This difference is important to understand. When you use a debit card, you are using your own money from your checking account, just as if you had written a check. When you use a credit card, you are borrowing money from the bank, which you will need to pay back.

When you use a debit card, the funds are almost immediately withdrawn from your checking account.

Unlike a paper check, which can take up to several days before the money is withdrawn from your account (called *float*), a debit card has almost no time delay. If you don't have the funds in your bank account to cover your debit card purchase, it is the same as writing an overdraft paper check and will result in an overdraft fee. The merchant who accepted your check may also charge you a similar fee to cover their expenses of dealing with your overdraft. Worse yet, should you overdraw your account by using your debit card, and then several other outstanding checks arrive after that, each check will also be assessed an overdraft fee. All of these charges can easily add up to a very large amount of money.

On the other hand, when you use a credit card, you are getting a loan from the bank or other card issuer. A credit card allows you to complete your purchase regardless of the money you have in your checking account (provided you don't exceed your credit card limit). And, if you pay off your credit card balance within the grace period, you can avoid paying any interest charges.

Other credit card and debit card differences

Credit cards do not use a PIN; instead, they require a signature, provided you are making a purchase in person. If you make a purchase online, no signature is required. The merchant that sells you the merchandise online has to bear the risk that without a signature; you may not have authorized the use of your credit card. Therefore, the merchant bears any losses associated with the unauthorized use of your card and not you.

Debit cards are most often used at *ATMs*, or *Automatic Teller Machines,* to withdraw cash from your checking account. Many times there will be — yes, you guessed it — a fee for this service. Banks sometimes have lower fees, or even no fees, provided you use their ATMs. Other ATMs, such as you might find at a convenience store, can have very high fees. These may run as high as several dollars per card use.

Should you choose to use a credit card instead of a debit card at an ATM, the cash you withdraw does not come from your checking account. Instead, it results in another type of loan called a "cash advance," for which the bank charges still another fee, perhaps $10 or more, for each cash advance. And, as with all loans, you will have to pay interest on the money you borrow.

Try not to use your credit card at the ATM
to get a cash advance.

Be smart: know your credit card protections

The use of credit cards, having been around longer than debit cards, is covered by an older federal law called the 1975 Fair Credit Billing Act. This law provides a number of protections superior to those available to debit card users, provided they follow proper procedures. What is covered? The following is a list summarized by the Federal Trade Commission:

- Unauthorized charges, including those resulting from lost or stolen credit cards;
- Charges listing the wrong date or amount;

- Charges for goods and services you didn't accept or that weren't delivered as agreed;
- Math errors;
- Failure of the credit card issuer to post payments or other credits, such as returns;
- Failure to send bills to your current address;
- Charges for which you have asked for an explanation or written proof of purchase.

In general, your loss from unauthorized credit card use is limited to $50.

In order to take advantage of these protections, you must notify the bank or card issuer in writing at the address given for billing inquiries on your credit card statement. You should include your name, address, account number, and a description of the billing error. The letter must be sent within 60 days after you receive the first statement showing the error. Finally, the letter must be sent certified mail, return receipt requested. You may notify your bank or credit card issuer by phone, and it is highly recommended that you do; however, only a written notice will preserve your rights under the law.

Be smart some more: debit card protections

Your losses arising from wrongful use of your debit cards, on the other hand, are covered by a later law, the Electronic Fund Transfer Act of 1978, and the protections are more limited. First, if your debit card is lost or stolen and you notify the bank before it is used for any unauthorized transactions, you won't suffer any loss. In order to limit your loss to $50 as with credit cards, you must notify your bank within two business days of discovering an unauthorized transaction, whether from a lost or stolen card, or arising from other charges and errors as listed for credit cards. Should you wait up to sixty days, your potential losses under this law may be as high as $500. Beyond sixty days, your losses could be unlimited, including all of the money in your account along with all lines of credit attached to that account.

Once again, the notice has to be in writing to enjoy the full protection of the law. However, telephone notification is highly recommended, as it will limit, as much as possible, any additional unauthorized transactions.

After you notify the bank, they have up to ten business days to conduct an investigation. During that time, you may have no access to your account. Think about that! You could potentially lose access to your checking account to pay any of your other bills. If the bank takes longer to investigate, they have to provide you with a temporary credit pending the outcome of their review.

When you use a debit card, or other electronic fund transfer, you cannot stop payment for defective merchandise or for merchandise that was never delivered.

With paper checks and credit cards you can withhold payment until the situation is resolved with the merchant. When you use a debit card, the merchant keeps your money, and it is up to you to get it back.

Should you use a debit card for the purchase of such things as gasoline or a deposit on a rental car, you may be surprised when the merchant places a *hold*, or a temporary restriction, on the use of some of your money. The idea behind this action is that the merchant does not know the exact amount of your purchase when the card is swiped through a card reader, so they place a hold on an amount in your checking account funds which they believe will cover your potential charges. In most cases, this hold is for more than the purchase in order to protect the merchant from any possible fraud or unauthorized use of your card. For a rental car deposit, the hold could amount to hundreds of dollars. This hold stays in place until the exact amount of the purchase is known, which could take a couple of days. If during this time you choose to use your debit card thinking you have access to your full balance, you will overdraft your account.

Recent changes to credit card laws

As we have discussed any number of times, fees are a way of life and are becoming more so every day. In fact, in 2009 some members of Congress felt that credit card fees and charges had gotten out of hand, so they enacted a new law called the *Credit Card Accountability,*

Responsibility and Disclosure Act or CARD Act of 2009.
Under the provisions of this act, credit card users now
have some new protections.

- Late payment fees are limited to $25 unless one
  of your last six payments was late, in which case
  your fee may be up to $35.

- Your credit card issuer cannot charge you an
  inactivity fee—meaning a charge if you do not
  use your card.

- Your credit card issuer cannot charge you a late
  fee greater than your minimum payment. For
  example, they cannot charge a $25 late fee for a
  $10 minimum payment.

- Often, along with a late fee, card issuers will
  also increase the interest rate they will charge
  on your credit card balance. In the past, this
  increase applied to your entire credit card balance.
  Now, the increase is limited to new charges only
  and must be reevaluated every six months to
  determine if the rate increase is still justified.

- Credit card issuers cannot allow you to exceed
  your limit (and charge you a penalty fee) unless
  you specifically agree in writing.

Why risk it: overdraft protection

One way you can avoid overdraft fees is to link your
checking account to a line of credit. This *overdraft
protection,* or line of credit, functions much like a
credit card loan, but without some of the protections.
Banks offer overdraft protection to cover the amount

of any overdrafts arising from writing checks or making debit card charges which overdraw your checking account. This coverage has an upper limit based upon how much the bank believes you can eventually pay back. This loan kicks in automatically when you write an overdraft check or make a debit charge resulting in an overdraft.

By now, you have probably guessed there is a fee attached to using overdraft protection. There will be a fee to activate the protection each time it is used, along with interest charges on any amounts loaned to your account. However, the total cost to you will be much less than typical overdraft fees and penalties, and the merchant who has accepted your overdraft check or debit card will be paid in full.

In light of the limited protections afforded by debit cards, their use should be limited to cash withdrawals at ATMs, or at most small "cash and carry" purchases. Moreover, if you pay off your credit card balances within the grace period, you will incur no more costs from using your credit card than if you had used your debit card.

The one instance for which you should never use your debit card is to make online purchases.

You might potentially wipe out your checking account balance along with any overdraft protection. There are simply too many unscrupulous merchants on the Internet to take the risk. And, if you fail to notice the charges in time, you could suffer a complete loss of all of your money.

The latest and the greatest: prepaid debit cards

A popular option for those without a checking account is the *prepaid debit card.* Instead of withdrawing money from your checking account, these cards require you to pay money up front for a card with a face value of $25, $100, and even $500. You, then, use the card until the money is exhausted. Some cards allow you to reload the balance, provided you again pay up front. Often, these cards have a lot of fees—some of which are obvious and some not so much. They almost all require a so-called activation fee, ranging from $10 to $100, along with a host of other charges including ATM fees, balance inquiry fees, monthly maintenance fees, inactivity fees, and even customer service fees.
There are almost no protections for the consumer with prepaid debit cards as provided with bank-issued debit and credit cards. Unscrupulous, prepaid-debit-card issuers can tack on fees for most anything and set the amounts for as much as they like. Should you use a prepaid debit card? Definitely not if you already have a checking account at a bank. In other cases, if you choose a reputable card issuer, it may be cheaper to pay the fees from a prepaid debit card instead of the monthly maintenance fees associated with a checking account. However, establishing a checking account with a bank builds your credit history, a key factor

underlying your credit score, while a prepaid debit card does nothing in that regard.

Check and not-a-check: e-checks

Now that you're armed with a solid understanding of debit and credit cards, some of the other electronic fund transfer services should be easier to understand. First up is *e-checks*, or electronic checks. Some merchants, such as Walmart, scan your paper check, thereby creating an electronic check. This allows them to send the information from your paper check to your bank electronically, much the same as if you had used your debit card. The merchant will *void* your paper check, or mark it to prevent its reuse, and then return it to you. This electronic conversion of your check allows the merchant faster access to the money in your checking account. So, if you think that by writing a check you have a couple of days to make a deposit to cover it, think again. You should keep the voided check in case of an error, as there won't be a photocopy of it in your monthly bank statement.

The penalty for being lazy: automatic withdrawal

Another common banking service is *automatic withdrawal,* or the electronic transfer of money from your checking account to another account on a recurring basis, requiring no action on your part. Utilities, phone companies, cable and satellite TV, just to mention a few, all encourage you to use automatic withdrawal.

"Just sign up once and forget about the hassles of paying monthly bills," they claim. To initiate the process, you sign an agreement authorizing these businesses to make direct withdrawals from your checking or credit card account to pay their monthly bills. It can be a convenience, but it also carries a degree of risk. First among these is the risk that an automatic withdrawal will hit your checking account at the wrong time, resulting in an overdraft.

The bigger risk with these agreements lies in trying to stop them, should you run into a problem. If you have an automatic withdrawal agreement and, for whatever reason, there is an error or a disputed charge, you cannot ask the bank to stop future withdrawals. These agreements are between you and the merchant, not between you and the bank. The bank cannot interfere with the agreement as they were not a part of it. The bank is only acting on your instructions as authorized in the automatic withdrawal agreement. In order to stop automatic withdrawals, you must get the merchant to agree to stop billing you. If they are unscrupulous, which is possible with some Internet businesses, you may have a very difficult challenge trying to do this. Worse yet, even if you close your account, the automatic withdrawals can still be held against you.

If you can't end the agreement, you can stop automatic withdrawal payments — but only one at a time — and the stop-payment order is only good for one transaction at a time. Here is how the process works, according to the US Treasury:

"To stop payment, you will need to notify the bank at least three business days before the transaction is scheduled to be made (the automatic withdrawal). Notice may be made orally or in writing. However, if the notice is made orally, the bank may require you to follow up with written notice within 14 days. If you don't provide written verification of the oral notice when required, the oral stop payment order ceases to be effective."

On top of all this, your bank may charge you a fee for each stop-payment order. You should be very careful with automatic withdrawal agreements, limiting their use to only those businesses and individuals whom you trust. Even better, don't enter into these agreements in the first place.

A much better way: online bill payment

Instead of automatic withdrawal, you should use your bank's electronic bill payment system, which is termed a *"push"* process, as opposed to automatic withdrawals, which is a *"pull"* process. As we just discussed, automatic withdrawal allows a merchant to pull money from your account whenever they elect to bill you. In a push process, you must first authorize any withdrawals from your checking account. In essence, you push the money out of your account.

This banking service may have slightly different

names, but it is commonly called *online bill payment.*
Your bank will require you to provide the payment
details for a list of merchants and service providers
with whom you have ongoing business dealings. Then
the bank will release funds only after you receive a bill
from the merchant, which you have approved. Some
banks require you to manually enter billing amounts
and authorize each payment. Others have more auto-
mated systems. Whichever one you use, consider any
inconvenience as a small price to pay to protect your
bank account from unauthorized use.

PayPal

If you've ever purchased anything from eBay, you are
probably familiar with PayPal. It is yet another electronic fund transfer service, except that PayPal is not
associated with any bank. Instead, PayPal acts as a
middle man between your bank and a seller. This
service offers a higher level of protection of your
financial information because the seller never has
access to your checking or credit card information.
Unlike a purchase at a store, where you hand over your
credit card to the seller or swipe it through their
terminal, this never happens with PayPal. Instead, you
give your financial information to PayPal. They, in
turn, conduct the transaction with the seller on your
behalf. As a consumer, PayPal costs you nothing extra
as all PayPal expenses are paid for by the seller.

To set up a PayPal account, you must give them access

to either a credit card or to your bank account. While there is a definite benefit to keeping your financial information hidden from potentially unscrupulous sellers, you should know that PayPal is not a bank, nor is it regulated like a bank. This means you are relying on PayPal to do the right thing. Their policies covering payment disputes and your exposure to potential losses are left to their discretion.

Because PayPal is a fact of life for many online purchases, the best course of action is to link only your credit card and not your bank account to this service. In this way you can still rely on the protections afforded by credit card laws, even if you act through a middle man, such as PayPal.

Balancing your electronic checking accounts

Once again, we return to the basic task of keeping track of all of those purchases which withdraw money from your checking account: debit cards, electronic checks, automatic withdrawals, and online bill pay. Here's the good news: The plain, old check register, covered in the last chapter, can easily accommodate these transactions. You simply treat all electronic transactions, such as debit card charges, as if they were paper checks. You use a separate line to record the date, payee, and amount for each one. While there is no check number to record, there may be a transaction number on your purchase receipt. Likewise, you should record the date and amount of all ATM with-drawals the same way, along with any associated ATM fees.

When you balance your checking account with these electronic fund transfers included, you follow the same process as with paper checks. On your bank statement, electronic transfers are typically listed separately from your paper checks. You will need to compare your electronic charges, electronic deposits, and all associated fees on the bank statement with your personal check register, using the same four-step process for paper checks as outlined in the last chapter. That's all there is to it. One advantage of electronic charges is that they are nearly instantaneous. There will be few times, if any, where you have recorded a transaction that doesn't appear in your statement.

In this chapter, we covered the fundamentals of electronic banking by comparing both the characteristics and protections of debit cards, credit cards, electronic checks, automatic withdrawals, and online bill payment.

Prepaid debit cards allow people without checking accounts to use electronic funds transfer, but they also incur more fees and have almost no consumer protections. Non-bank services such as PayPal act as the middle man between you and a merchant, providing you with the increased protection of your financial information. However, they are not a bank and their consumer protections are limited to their own policies.

Terms covered in Chapter 10

- **Electronic Funds Transfer**
- **PIN**
- **Float**
- **ATM**
- **Hold**
- **Automatic Withdrawal**
- **E-check**
- **Void**
- **PayPal**
- **Push**
- **Pull**

Practical App: implied authority

Did you know that if you lend your credit card or debit card to a friend with instructions to buy a pizza and a beer but she buys an airline ticket to Hawaii instead, you can still be held responsible to pay for those charges? It's called *apparent authority*. If a merchant believes a cardholder, such as your friend, has your permission to use your card, then you are on the hook to make the payments. For a debit card, all you have to do is provide your friend with your PIN. When you do, you have given them permission to use your card to purchase anything they choose.

To protect your money, the best advice is to never let anyone use your credit or debit card. Period. Aloha.

11   Tax Savvy

Taxes, taxes and more taxes

As a United States citizen, you will pay taxes for the rest of your life, so you should understand what they are and how your tax dollars are used. Then when you exercise your right to vote, you can make an informed decision about just how much you should pay in taxes and for what.

Many of the terms defined in this section regularly appear in the news as our leaders seek to stretch budgets to pay for all of the goods and services our government now provides or has promised to provide in the future.

Here is a quiz. See if you can guess which of these items is paid for using taxes collected in the United States.

Police protection	Military
Snow plowing	Airplane safety
Road building	National park rangers
School Teachers	GPS system
Parks	Community facilities

The answer is . . . all of the above, along with thousands of other goods and services. And who pays those taxes? Everyone who lives, works, or travels in the United States through sales taxes, income taxes, property taxes, payroll taxes, and literally thousands of others.

And how much do United States citizens pay in taxes? According to the *OECD, the Organization of Economic Cooperation and Development,* which regularly conducts surveys of the *tax burden,* or the total of all taxes collected by their member countries; in 2009 (the latest year for which statistics are available) the OECD survey showed that the total United States tax burden, across all levels of government, amounted to 24 percent of its *GDP,* or *Gross Domestic Product.* That means the equivalent of one-fourth of the value of the entire annual production of goods and services of the United States for that year was used by the government to provide services to its citizens.

US taxes versus other developed countries

It may come as a surprise to some, but our tax burden is relatively low as compared with some of the other OECD member countries shown in *Table 11.1.* However, you should also keep in mind that countries with higher rates often pay for goods and services for which the United States government does not pay, such as public healthcare for citizens under the age of sixty-five.

Table 11.1 2009 Tax Burden as a Percentage of GDP

Denmark	48.2
Sweden	46.4
Japan	28.1
Canada	31.1
France	41.9
Turkey	24.8
United States	24.0
Mexico	17.5
Chile	18.2
Average of OECD	33.7 %

Even more surprising, OECD analysis also indicates that the tax burden of its members through 2009 has fallen to the lowest levels since the 1990s. In 2007, for example, the burden was 35.4 percent, which then dropped to 34.8 percent in 2008, and then dropped again to 33.7 percent in 2009.

Deciding which goods and services should be paid for with taxes and which should be left for individuals to pay for on their own is a part of *tax policy*. The elected officials representing US citizens ultimately decide tax policy. Often a matter of intense debate, the current priorities for US federal tax policy are shown on the following page in Table 11.2.

Table 11.2 2012 United States Federal Expenditures

	$ Trillions	% of Total
Healthcare	.8	21
Pensions	.8	21
Education	.2	5
Defense	.9	24
Welfare	.5	13
Other	.6	16
Total	$ 3.8	100 %

usgovernementspending.com

By way of explanation, healthcare expenses cover mostly services for senior and low-income citizens at present. Pensions include retirement benefits for government employees. Education expenses include mainly administration costs and some direct funds made available to states which fund the majority of education costs.

Off the deep end: deficits

There is one more critical piece of information you should know about taxes and government expenditures. Just as individuals borrow money to pay for goods and services they can't immediately afford, the United States does the same thing. Known as the national debt, this is the money we, as a nation, spend by borrowing money.

According to the Bureau of Public Debt of the United States Treasury, as of September 2011, the national debt stood at $14.7 trillion dollars, or approximately $47,000 for every US citizen. That amount is equivalent to one hundred iPads, or two brand new cars, or perhaps five to ten vacations per person. For every year in which the federal government spends (called *outlays*) more than it takes in (called *receipts*), the difference (called a *deficit*) adds to the national debt.

For over a decade, the federal government has continued to spend more than it takes in at an ever-increasing rate. According to the Financial Management Service Bureau of the United States Treasury, as of the end of September 2011, our annual deficit stood at $1.3 trillion dollars. Decreasing our deficit through various plans of increasing taxes and lowering government expenditures is once again a matter of debate.

I'll know it when I see it: taxes defined

Let's first define a *tax* and then look at some of the more common ones.

> *A tax is a financial charge levied by the government on individuals and property.*

Payment of taxes is not voluntary; rather, it is the responsibility of every United States citizen to pay for the goods and services provided by the government. The US Constitution under Article 1, Section 8 grants Congress the power to tax, as well as the power to enforce its collection.

Although there are hundreds, if not thousands of

taxes, almost everyone is familiar with the four more common ones: payroll taxes, sales taxes, income taxes, and property taxes. All of these are based upon a *tax rate*, or a percentage, applied against a taxable amount, such as your income or paycheck. Let's look as payroll taxes as an example.

Paying taxes as you go: payroll taxes

Anyone who has had a job is familiar with *payroll taxes*. There are two different types of payroll taxes. First, there are taxes employers collect from the employee by withholding money from the employee's paycheck, and then there are taxes which the employer pays out of its own money as its obligation arising from having employees. The first type of tax, called a *withholding tax,* is used to fund the employee's future tax obligations for federal and state income taxes, along with their future *Social Security* and *Medicare* benefits. Social Security is a pension payable to qualifying taxpayers starting when they reach a minimum age of sixty-two. As of the date of this publication, the tax rate for the employee is set by the federal government at 6.2 percent of wages. Medicare withholding pays for government-paid healthcare for taxpayers over the age of sixty-five, and the employee's portion is currently set at 1.45 percent of wages. Together these two taxes are called *FICA*, or *Federal Insurance Contributions Act*, taxes.

The second kind of tax, paid from the employer's own

funds, pays for state and federal unemployment taxes to cover an employee's unemployment benefits along with the employer's share of the employee's FICA taxes. In essence the employer pays its share of FICA in an amount equal to the amount paid by the employee. In total, taxes for Social Security amount to 12.4 percent of the employee's wages, and taxes for Medicare amount to 2.9 percent of the employee's wages.

For those who are interested, the other common taxes, sales, property and income, are covered in more detail in Appendix A.

Another form: payroll tax withholding Form W4

While an employee cannot change the amount of withholding for FICA or unemployment taxes, they can change the amount withheld for federal and state income taxes. This is accomplished using a *W4* form (one for federal taxes and one for state taxes). Every employee fills out a W4 form upon starting a new job. On this form, employees select a number of *allowances* to arrive at a withholding amount that ideally matches the amount needed to cover their future federal and state income taxes.

It's still my money: tax avoidance

From the prior discussion, it is obvious that taxes play a significant role in how much money you get to keep from your earnings. While it is the responsibility of every US citizen to pay taxes, this does not mean that you have to pay any more tax than necessary. Paying the minimum amount of taxes permitted by law is called *tax avoidance* and is a legitimate way to stretch your dollars. How this is accomplished is beyond the scope of an introductory money guide, but you should know there is an entire industry of tax professionals specializing in minimizing tax payments.

In this chapter, we have defined taxes and how tax collections are spent. Payroll taxes have been explained in some detail. It is important to understand taxes as you will spend a significant portion of your money on them, now and throughout your life. Ultimately, you as a citizen decide, through your vote, how much and for what purpose these taxes will be used.

Terms covered in Chapter 11

- **Tax Burden**
- **OECD**
- **Deficits**
- **National Debt**
- **Payroll Tax**
- **FICA**
- **Social Security**
- **Medicare**
- **W4**
- **Allowances**

Practical App: fatten your paycheck

Many believe that getting a tax refund from their income taxes is a good thing. In fact, it is money you have allowed the government to use, without any compensation to you. Had you instead used that same money to pay down credit card debt, you would have saved yourself some interest charges. Or, you might have deposited it in savings to earn interest income.

How do you reduce your tax refund and keep more of your income? By changing your W4 form. On the W4 form there is a worksheet portion that can help you calculate the proper withholding amount from your paycheck. If you find the worksheet doesn't provide the result which best matches your withholding to your estimated income taxes, you are free to increase or decrease the number of allowances to suit your needs. Instead of waiting until the following April to get your money back, the money can be yours to use each month as you receive your paycheck.

12 Compound Interest and Loans

As you will recall from Chapter 1, a loan is a particular type of debt involving money. Banks and other lenders make loans in order to earn interest, which is a charge the borrower pays to the lender for the use of the lender's money.

The amount of the loan on which you pay interest is called the principal.

Loan interest charges are calculated by multiplying the loan principal by the loan interest rate. This rate is stated as some percentage for a given period of time, such as 1 percent per month or 15 percent per year. This total, in turn, is multiplied by the number of time periods (usually months) required by the borrower to pay the loan principal back to the lender. The mathematical formula is as follows:

Simple Interest = Principal x Interest rate x No. of periods

For example, let's say the loan principal is $100 and the monthly interest rate is 1 percent per month. The simple interest due after five months would be calculated as follows:

$100 principal x 1% interest rate x 5 months = $5.00

The interest charge calculated in this example is called *simple interest*, as opposed to *compound interest*. Compound interest adds interest charges onto the principal at the end of each time period, usually monthly, and then charges interest on that amount. In other words, interest charges due the lender from one period are added onto the principal for the next period. Interest is then calculated on that total and so on for as many periods as the borrower requires to pay back the principal. This is a powerful concept that, as a borrower, can either cost you a lot of money, or, as a saver, make you a lot of money.

Let's walk through how compound interest works. Using the above example, let's say the borrower decides not to make any payments to the lender for three months, choosing instead to pay off the loan completely at the end. For the first month, the lender calculates the total amount due from the borrower using simple interest:

$100 principal x 1% interest x 1 month = $1.00

For the second month, the lender adds the interest charge from the first month onto the principal and then uses the simple interest rate formula to calculate the charge for the second month:

($100 principal + $1 interest from first month) x 1% interest rate x 1 month = $1.01

For the next month, the interest charges from the first two periods are added onto the principal, and again, the simple interest rate is applied as follows:

($100 principal + $2.01 interest from first two periods) x 1% interest x 1 month = $1.02

The interest charge for the first month of $1.00 is added to the charge for the second month of $1.01 along with the third month of $1.02 for a grand total of $3.03. Had the lender used only simple interest, the borrower would have had to pay only $3.00, instead of $3.03 or $.03 more using compound interest.

This may not sound like much, but compound interest builds like a locomotive. When it leaves the station, it moves very slowly, but after a period of time it can take out anything in its path. Using the above example, let's see what happens to the total principal after fifty years (600 months), again comparing simple and compound interest rates.

Simple interest charges

Total interest charge due after 50 years = 1% interest x $100 principal x 600 months = **$600.00**

Compound interest charges

Total interest charge due after 50 years = $((1 + .01)^{600})$ interest x $100 principal) = **$39,158.34**

Don't worry if you can't follow the calculations in this example as they can get complicated when computing compound interest. However, do note the difference in the totals. With compound interest, that extra one cent per month at the beginning ends up making a difference of $38,558.34 in the end! This gives you some idea of how credit card balances can get so out of control when the borrower makes only minimum payments.

Your BFF: annual percentage rate

Typically, lenders express interest charges for a period of one year called *APR*, or *annual percentage rate*. However, this annual rate may differ depending upon whether they use simple or compound interest, as the following two calculations show. Both are based upon a monthly interest rate of 1 percent.

Simple interest APR = 1% monthly rate x 12 = 12%

Compound interest APR = $(1\% \text{ monthly rate})^{12}$ = 12.68%

As you can see, two loans may have the same 1 percent per month interest rate, but the one that uses compounding will always have a greater APR than the one using simple interest. Lenders are required to show the APR for their loans so that borrows can make comparisons between lenders based upon the annual cost of borrowing. Be forewarned, for some loans, lenders can choose to use either simple interest or compound interest. And, as you already know, simple interest will understate the true cost of borrowing.

In addition, lenders must also include any loan fees or other loan-related expenses in the APR calculation. For example, a $100 loan with a 1 percent monthly rate of interest (using compound interest) without any fees has a 12.68 percent APR as shown earlier, while the same loan with a $10 fee up front would have a first year APR of 22.68 percent. The loan fee is treated the same as if it were an additional interest charge in the first year.

Compound interest and savings accounts

Now, consider what would have happened if you had deposited that $100 from the above example into your savings instead of borrowing it. Let's say you invested it for twenty years at 1 percent per month interest or 12.68 percent APR. At the end, you would have over ten times more than what you deposited, or a total of $1,089.25. In essence, you have switched places with the bank, and they now pay you interest for borrowing your money. Of course, 12.68 percent APR is a rather high interest rate, which most banks don't pay for savings; however, the power of compounding is still a powerful force even with interest rates of 3, 4, or 5 percent, providing you leave the money alone for a long enough period of time.

All about loans

As we discussed way back in Chapter 2, loans can be classified in a variety of ways. And, to make things even more confusing, the same loan may fall into different classifications, depending upon which of its characteristics is the focus. For example, one of the broadest classifications is secured and unsecured loans.

> *A secured loan gives the lender the right to take property from the borrower should the borrower fail to make timely loan payments.*

Such property can include boats, cars, and real estate. A car loan is a common type of secured loan providing the lender the right to take the borrower's car should she fail to repay the lender as agreed. The car, called *collateral*, provides additional protection for the lender. Generally, lenders charge lower loan interest rates for secured loans.

Unsecured loans are just the opposite of secured loans. For this type of loan, the lender relies solely upon the borrower's past financial history, i.e. their credit score, and their promise to meet their loan obligations. These loans include personal loans, credit card loans, and student loans. Without collateral, the interest rate for unsecured loans is higher than for secured loans.

Many secured loans can also be classified as *conven-*

tional loans, which are a loan type with a fixed amount of principal borrowed at the beginning of the loan term, with fixed payments. Again, a car loan is a good example. The borrower borrows the entire principal up front to purchase a car and then makes equal payments over the life of the loan. However, not all conventional loans are secured loans. Those without collateral are referred to as unsecured conventional loans because they share all of the other characteristics of conventional loans, except for collateral.

I've heard that line before: line of credit

Unlike a conventional loan, a *revolving line* or *line of credit* does not restrict the amount of principal to a one-time, up front amount. In this instance, the loan principal may decrease or increase many times over the life of the loan up to a maximum, predetermined limit.

Likewise, the payments will change based upon the amount of outstanding principal. These payments are typically calculated as a percentage of the principal balance plus interest charges. Because these are unsecured loans, the interest rate can be quite high, and unlike conventional loans, the interest rate can even be raised should the lender determine that the borrower is a credit risk.

A loan for the long term: mortgages

A mortgage, which is also a conventional loan and a secured loan, is a loan for which the collateral is real estate, typically a home. Because real estate seldom loses value over long periods of time, the loan term can be for a very long period as well, often fifteen to thirty years or longer. The interest rate for mortgages is also lower than for other types of loans because the value of the collateral is more predictable, again seldom losing value as a car or boat would.

Lenders will not lend money for a mortgage exceeding the value of the real estate collateral. In fact, the loan amount of a mortgage is usually limited to an amount equal to only 75–80 percent of full value. As an example, a home worth $100,000 would qualify for a mortgage of $75,000 to $80,000.

As a conventional loan, a mortgage has fixed, equal payments. The amount of each payment is calculated in such a way that the loan balance will be completely paid off by the end of the loan term using a mathematical formula called a *loan amortization*. While every mortgage payment is fixed in total, early loan payments pay mostly interest charges, while the later ones pay mostly principal. For example, a thirty-year loan of $100,000, with a fixed interest rate of 5 percent, would have equal monthly payments of $536.82. The first payment includes $416.67 in interest and $120.15

in principal. By way of comparison, the last payment includes $1.91 in interest payments and $534.91 in principal payments. As you can see, the earlier loan payments do not make much headway against the principal. In the next chapter, we will see how this loan amortization causes problems in student loans.

In this chapter, we covered simple and compound interest. Don't worry if the mathematics escapes you. The important point to remember is how these concepts affect your loan payments. Higher interest rates, because of compounding, can lead to very large increases in loan balances over time. We also examined a few of the more common loan types which you will encounter throughout your life. Lines of credit, conventional loans, and mortgages are a few examples.

Terms covered in Chapter 12

- **Principal**
- **Simple Interest**
- **Compound Interest**
- **Collateral**
- **Conventional Loan**
- **Line of Credit**
- **Mortgage**
- **Loan Amortization**
- **APR**

Practical App: credit card shopping

Take a look at your credit card statement. In it, you will find important information about your credit card debt. Try to find your APR. What are the penalties for a late payment? Now go on the Internet and see if you can find a credit card with a better APR or one with a longer grace period. You may want to consider transferring your outstanding balance to another card with better terms. One caution: if you do find cards with better terms, only apply for one or two. An excessive number of credit applications can negatively impact your credit score.

13 Student Loan Savvy

Student loans are loans made either by the federal government, called *direct loans,* or by banks and credit unions, called *private loans.* Their purpose is to help students pay for college tuition, books and living expenses. These loans are also available for community colleges, as well as trade and technical schools.

Some federal student loans are *subsidized,* in that the US government pays some of the loan costs in order to offer lower interest rates and better repayment terms. You must be a US citizen with a valid Social Security number to qualify for a federal loan.

Reading, writing and repayment

Student loans belong to a select group of obligations that are very difficult to escape repaying. While most other loans can be cancelled, or *discharged* through bankruptcy, student loans are an exception. These loans can potentially remain with you for the rest of your life. It is, therefore, extremely important to understand your obligations as defined in their *loan provisions* as you will be held accountable if you should fail to fulfill them,

As with all debt, and especially so with student loans, the best advice is to borrow as little as possible, regardless of whether it is from the government or private lenders. You can accomplish this by reducing college expenses as much as possible in the first place. Ask yourself if the income from your future job will support the expense of an education at an exclusive college or university? Can you substitute lower-cost credits from advanced placement or community-college courses for the more expensive credits from a four-year degree school?

There are many other cost-saving strategies you might want to consider before you take out a student loan. While such strategies are beyond the scope of this book, a variety of resources are available to help you (see recommended reading).

Next, you should exhaust all non-loan financial aid, including Federal Supplemental Educational Opportunity Grants, Pell Grants, TEACH Grants, Federal Work Study, and scholarships, to mention a few. These forms of financial aid do not require repayment; however, there are also strict requirements as to who may qualify to receive such financial assistance.

Finally, if you must borrow money, you should apply for federal loans first as these will generally have the lowest interest rates and the best repayment terms.

The cavalry arrives: federal student loans

The majority of direct student loans are made through the federal Department of Education.

Stafford loans, subsidized Stafford loans, and PLUS loans are the three most common federal loan programs.

The amounts that can be borrowed under each loan program are capped depending upon whether students are graduates or undergraduates, living as dependents, and their year in school. All direct loans offer a fixed low-interest rate and fixed payments that begin after a grace period, usually six months after graduation.

The PLUS loan, or Parent Loan Undergraduate Student, is a direct loan made to parents of undergraduate students. The parents must qualify based upon an acceptable credit history and capacity to make repayment. The student must be under 24, single, and have no dependents. These loans have a higher interest rate (currently 7.9 percent) than the other two direct loan programs. In addition, there is a fee (currently in the amount of 4 percent of principal) assessed as loan amounts are disbursed.

Stafford loans are made only to students. The subsidized Stafford loan differs from a standard Stafford loan in that all of the interest charges are paid by the government while the student is in school. However, only low-income students with a demonstrated financial need can qualify for a subsidized Stafford loan. Students and parents should understand one caution about direct loans. Repayment can be triggered should a student leave school or at such time as a student's course load drops to half-time. However, should either of these events occur and the student takes corrective action within a six-month grace period, then repayment will again be deferred until after graduation.

Under the *standard plan*, once repayment starts, the student has ten years to repay the loan through fixed monthly payments with a minimum of at least $50. There are a number of modifications available to this standard plan, which can increase the time to repay the loan along with an accompanying decrease in the payment amount. These modifications go by names such as Income Based Repayment, Graduated Payments, and Income Contingent Repayments. However, all of these modifications will increase the total amount a student will ultimately have to repay—much like lower credit card payments will increase the total of credit card debt as discussed in Chapter 3.

Stafford loans, unlike subsidized Stafford loans merely defer interest payments (adding them onto the loan balance) while the student is in school. As discussed within the compound interest topic from the previous chapter, interest charges piled on top of interest charges can add up quickly leaving many students buried under a mountain of debt.

It is possible in some very limited circumstances to qualify for student loan cancellation, meaning a student does not have to pay off the loan. The loan-forgiveness provisions require a lengthy repayment period first (ten or more years), accompanied by continuous employment in public service or a non-profit job. There are other cancellation options as well, but qualifying for them can be equally difficult.

You cannot escape the consequences of default

You should understand that failure to repay these direct federal student loans, called a *loan default*, will result in severe penalties. Following is a list of consequences published on the *Federal Student Aid* website:

If you default:

- We will require you to immediately repay the entire unpaid amount of your loan.

- We may sue you, take all or part of your federal and state tax refunds and other federal or state payments, and/or garnish your wages so that your employer is required to send us part of your salary to pay off your loan.

- We will require you to pay reasonable collection fees and costs, plus court costs and attorney fees.

- You may be denied a professional license.

- You will lose eligibility for other federal student

aid and assistance under most federal benefit programs.

- You will lose eligibility for loan deferments.
- We will report your default to national consumer reporting agencies (credit bureaus).

Loan deferment and forbearance

Provided you qualify, the government may grant a temporary halt to your payments through either a deferment or forbearance.

A deferment is a period of time in which payments are suspended. It is granted only in special situations such as re-enrollment in school, unemployment, military service, or economic hardship.

If you have a subsidized Stafford loan, the government will make your interest payments for as long as your loan is deferred.

If you can't qualify for loan deferment, you can still receive *forbearance,* during which time the government will temporarily halt your payments (in one-year increments) for up to three years.

Forbearance is granted to those not qualified to receive a deferment. Forbearance provides the same payment-suspension benefits; however, all interest charges continue to accrue until loan payments resume.

Regardless of whether you have a subsidized loan or

other direct loan, during loan forbearance the government will not make your interest payments — all interest charges will be added on to the loan principal.

Let's look at the financial consequences of loan forbearance. Consider the following two cases shown in Exhibit 1: Case 1 is for a student who has an initial loan balance of $25,000 with an interest rate of 3.4 percent, and Case 2 is for the same student with an interest rate of 6.8 percent. The former rate is the one currently in effect, while the latter is the one which is likely to go into effect in the near future. Let's also suppose that in both cases, the student has made payments for two years of a ten-year loan-repayment schedule. Then at that point, the student opts for a three-year loan forbearance.

Exhibit 13.1 Loan Forbearance

	Case 1	Case 2
Interest Rate:	3.4%	6.8%
Original loan balance:	$25,000	$25,000
Loan balance after 2 years (at start of forbearance)	$20,655	$21,257
Monthly loan payment	$ 246	$ 287
Interest added on to principal during forbearance period	$2,215	$4,795
New principal balance at the end of forbearance	$22,870	$26,052

Note that in both cases the loan balance after the forbearance period is greater than the balance at the beginning owing to the interest charges incurred during that period of time — $2,215 additional interest in Case 1 and $4,795 additional interest in Case 2. Note also that the higher the interest rate, the greater the principal balance increases. In fact, in Case 2, the loan balance is greater than the original loan amount, more than canceling out two years of payments.

Loan forbearance can be a painfully expensive price to pay for short-term financial relief, much like only making minimum credit card payments. You should make every effort to keep up with interest payments during loan forbearance so as to at least not lose ground against principal repayment.

Another day another loan: Perkins loans

Perkins loans are low-interest (currently 5 percent) government loans made to students with exceptional financial need. Unlike Stafford and PLUS loans, these loans are made through the financial aid office of the college or university who also administers the loan. There are no loan fees, but there are restrictions as to the amount that can be borrowed at any given time. These loans have a grace period after graduation of nine months before payments commence. All of the cautions mentioned above regarding default, deferment, and forbearance apply equally to Perkins Loans.

Lots of choices: private loans

Private student loans resemble direct loans except they are made by banks, credit unions, and other lenders instead of the government. In order to qualify for these loans, you must have an acceptable credit history. One of the largest private lenders is Sallie Mae, a government lender recently turned private. Unlike direct student loans from the government, private lenders generally charge more fees — and higher fees — for loan modifications, such as deferment, forbearance, or other changes in loan repayment terms.

As with government student loans, private student loans can be just as difficult, if not impossible, to discharge in bankruptcy. Should you default, however, private lenders have fewer tools that they can use to make collections,

A college education has become so expensive that many students need private student loans on top of their government loans to pay for it all. Once again, you should understand the loan terms thoroughly before you borrow, regardless of the lender.

Student loans are typically young adults' first significant debt. The benefits of a college education have to be weighed against the large costs required to obtain it. It is not enough to simply believe everything will work out. It is imperative to treat these loans with respect for the significant obligation they represent as they will be with you for a very long time.

In this chapter, we touched upon various types of student loans. The three most common government loan programs are Stafford loans, subsidized Stafford loans and PLUS loans. Private lenders such as Sallie Mae also make student loans; however, their loan terms may not be as borrower friendly. It is recommended that you explore all potential government-based financial aid before borrowing from a private lender.

Terms covered in Chapter 13

- **Stafford Loans**
- **Subsidized Stafford Loans**
- **PLUS Loans**
- **Discharge through Bankruptcy**
- **Default**
- **Deferment**
- **Forbearance**
- **Perkins Loans**
- **Private Loans**
- **Sallie Mae**

Practical App: college shopping

It's never too early to explore just how much a four-year college education will cost. You might want to consider state colleges and their local extensions as part of your cost comparison. Many times, local extensions offer a cheaper alternative than the main campus, and the credits will be accepted should you decide to transfer later in your education. Moreover, some community colleges also have agreements with state colleges for full credit transfers and may be an even more affordable alternative.

Appendix A   More About Taxes

Besides the payroll taxes covered in Chapter 11, the other most common US taxes are sales taxes, income taxes and property taxes. We will explore each of these in more depth in this appendix.

Sales taxes

Anyone who has made a purchase at a store is familiar with *sales tax*.

A sales tax is a tax paid by a consumer for goods and services purchased from a retailer.

The retailer collects the tax at the point of purchase (the time and place when a person or business pays for and takes possession of an item purchased), and then sends those tax collections to the Department of Revenue for the state in which the purchase was made. In essence, the merchant is the tax collector of the sales tax.

Generally, this tax only applies to the sales of tangible personal property, or TPP, which refers to property that can be seen, weighed, measured, touched, or otherwise perceived by the senses. TPP does not include real estate, or real property, which is legally considered a form of property distinct from personal property.

Sales taxes are calculated as a percentage of the retail

sales price. For example, if you make a $10 purchase in Colorado Springs, Colorado, the retailer would add 2.9 percent or $.29 onto the final sales price to pay for the state sales tax. On top of that, another 1 percent is added for county sales tax, and an additional 2.5 percent is added for city sales tax, resulting in a total of 6.4 percent, or a total of $.64 added onto the total purchase price (an additional 1% tax for road construction has been added for a total of 7.4%).

Forty-five states and the District of Columbia impose a sales tax on *TPP* and for certain services. While state and local governments impose a sales tax, the federal government does not.

Based upon US Constitutional principles, only state and local governments can levy a sales tax if they have some physical connection, or *nexus*, to the taxpayer. For example, consumers pay a sales tax in the city, county, and state in which they make a purchase. Based upon this principle, a neighboring state, say Utah, cannot collect sales taxes from a consumer who makes a purchase in Colorado.

Businesses as well as individuals pay sales taxes. In either case, it is the taxpayer who is responsible for paying sales tax. The retailer only collects it, and only if they too have a nexus with the taxpayer. The flip side of sales tax is a *use tax*. If the merchant who sells some item to you fails to collect sales tax, then you have to pay a use tax to your state based upon the same formula described above. Technically, online purchases for which sales taxes have not been collected by the seller are subject to use tax, which you, as the purchaser, are responsible to pay.

In recent years, online purchases have replaced more and more sales from local retailers. And, while these local retailers are required to collect sales taxes, online retailers are largely free of this requirement. As a result, state and local governments lose sales tax revenue, even though as just mentioned, consumers are responsible for paying sales tax for their online purchases. However, few actually do this.

In an effort to reclaim these lost taxes, state and local governments have expanded the definition of nexus for online businesses in such as way that forces many of them to collect sales taxes. As a result of these efforts, online businesses with any physical presence in a state, such as a store or warehouse, now have to collect state sales taxes. Some states have made even more aggressive efforts to collect sales taxes by broadening the definition of what they consider "a physical presence."

Not every sale is subject to a sales tax. There are a number of *exemptions*. One common exemption is for any TPP purchased by a retailer, which the retailer then resells to the final consumer. These *wholesale* sales are generally exempt from sales taxes.

Another common exemption is for services, such as a plumber fixing a leaky faucet or a carpenter installing a cabinet.

What does the government do with sales taxes? At the state level, the three biggest uses are for transportation (roads, bridges, and highways), public education, and aid to local governments. Local governments, such as cities and counties, use sales tax revenue for things such as police and fire protection, community swimming pools and community centers, salaries for government workers, and pensions for retired government workers.

April 15 dread: income taxes

Income taxes are another tax with which most everyone is familiar. This is a tax imposed by both the United States federal government, and most state governments on individual and business income. Federal income taxes are collected by the *IRS,* or *Internal Revenue Service*, a bureau of the US Treasury. State income taxes are collected by individual state *Departments of Revenue*. Most income taxes must be paid by April 15th on taxpayer income from the previous year ending December 31st.

Just as with sales tax, the amount of income tax is

determined by applying a percentage against some dollar amount, except in this case it is applied against annual income, instead of the retail price of a purchase. The federal income tax percentage, or *tax rate,* increases as your income increases. These increasing rates are applied in steps called *tax brackets.* As an example, *Table A1* shows the 2012 federal tax brackets for married taxpayers.

Table A1 Tax Tab;e

Taxable Income	Tax Rate
$0 – $16,999	10%
$17,000 – $69,999	15%
$70,000– $139,349	25%
$139,350 – $212,299	28%
$212,300 – $379,149	33%
$379,150 and above	35%

As you can see, the tax rate increases as income increases. The income tax is calculated by applying each rate in the order listed and then adding those amounts together. For example, the following is how the total tax for an income of $100,000 would be calculated.

Table A2 Income Tax Example

Income	Tax Rate	Income Tax Amount
$16,999	x 10% =	$ 1,699
$17,000 - $69,999	x 15% =	$ 7,950
$70,000 - $100,000	x 25% =	$ 7,500
Total		**$ 17,149**

The highest tax bracket percentage that can be applied to any given income, in this case 25 percent, is the *marginal tax rate* for that taxpayer. This means each additional dollar earned will be taxed at that rate. Again, notice this marginal tax rate is much higher for income over $69,000 than for incomes below $17,000.

A tax based upon an increasing marginal rate is called a progressive tax.

If all income, great or small, were taxed at only one rate, this would be an example of a *flat* tax. In the United States, we use progressive tax rates in the belief that those who have more resources should pay a greater share of the cost of government.

A tax system in which the opposite holds true and those who make less pay more than their share is called a *regressive* income tax system.

Not all income is subject to income taxes. Moreover, some states will tax income not taxed by the federal government, and vice versa. Which income is taxed and which is not is determined by *deductions,* or amounts allowed to be subtracted from income before tax rates are applied. Income after deductions are subtracted is called *net taxable income.* For example, taxpayers with incomes of $100,000 with deductions of $20,000 would have a net taxable income of $80,000, to which the rates of the tax table in Table A2 would then be applied.

There are a great number of deductions. However, some of the more common ones are a *standard deduction*, a *mortgage interest deduction*, and a *dependent deduction*. The standard deduction is an amount of income every US taxpayer is entitled to subtract from their income no matter how much they make. For example, in 2011, the standard deduction for single taxpayers was $5,800 and for married couples it was $11,600.

Taxpayers with a mortgage can claim a mortgage deduction allowing them to deduct the total of their annual interest expenses they have paid on their home loans. This deduction is one way that the government encourages home ownership by off-setting some of the cost of borrowing with a reduction in income tax.

Taxpayers who support family members, such as children or parents, can take advantage of a dependent deduction for each individual they support. There are a number of criteria that determines who can qualify as a family member and exactly what constitutes support, but children are generally considered dependents.

Finally, not all income taxes are based on the tax rates from tax tables, such as *Table A1*. For example, *capital gains,* or income resulting from the sale of property in excess of its purchase price, are taxed at a different rate than income earned from working at a job. In addition, the length of time the taxpayer owns the property before it is sold can also affect the tax rate.

As you can no doubt see, calculating income taxes can be complicated. One of the reasons is that government uses taxes as a means to influence how taxpayers make and spend their money. Taxing capital gains at a lower rate encourages taxpayers to use their money to make investments, such as for their homes, as opposed to spending money on cars and boats.

Influencing taxpayer spending is another part of tax policy, which Congress enacts based upon what it believes is in the best interests of the nation. As an example, at one time Congress enacted a luxury tax, or an extra tax on certain items like yachts and jewelry, which at that time they deemed to be a less desirable way for citizens to spend their money.

Taxes hit home: property taxes

Local governments, typically counties and cities, raise money by taxing real property, such as homes, office buildings, and land. These property taxes are used to pay for local protective services (police and fire); schools; streets and roads; and local government employees. The tax is based upon the *assessed value* of the property, which is derived from the sales values of similar nearby properties. Real estate assessments are typically performed every one to three years by a government employee called a *tax assessor*.

A tax rate, much like a sales tax and income tax, is applied against the assessed value of the property to arrive at the amount of the property tax. This tax rate, also called a *mil levy*, is a percentage applied to every $1,000 of property value. It is set by the local government at a level calculated to pay (along with other reveneues) for all of the services the local government intends to provide for the upcoming year.

For example, suppose a home has an assessed value of $100,000. If the property tax mil levy were 3.0, then for every $1,000 of value, the homeowner would pay three dollars. To calculate the total property tax, we divide the $100,000 assessed value by $1,000, which equals 100. The 100 is then multiplied by the $3.00 mill levy, and $300 is the resulting property tax. Property taxes are usually paid to the county treasurer, the government office responsible for both assessing property values and collecting property taxes.

Real property owners can, and often do, challenge

assessed values if they believe the value does not represent a fair value for their property. Every property-taxing authority—again, most often the county government—must provide a means for property owners to dispute their assessments.

In this appendix we have touched on several common taxes. These are taxes which most everyone will incur at some point in their lives. Understanding them is important because of their impact on your money as well as a part of your responsibility as a US citizen.

Bibliography

Besiger, Gregory. *Personal Finance for People Who Hate Personal Finance*. Liam Judge Pub., 2010. eBook.

Coleman, Aaron. *Winning with Money: The Budget Tool for People Who Hate Budgets*. Russell Media, 2011. eBook.

"Direct Stafford Loans." Student Aid. n.d. Web. 30 June 2012.

"FHA Requirements: Debt Guidelines." *FHA Requirements*. FHA n.d. Web. 6 June 2012.

Garmen, E. Thomas and Fogue, Raymond. *Personal Finance*. Ohio: South-Western College Pub., 2009. Print.

Holden, Lewis. "A Check is a Check: Whatever It's Printed On." *Blogs* Bankrate n.d. Web. 6 June 2012.

Kessel, Brent. *It's Not About the Money: Unlock Your Money Type to Achieve Spiritual and Financial Abundance*. New York: Harper Collins, 2008. Print.

Koblinger, Beth. *Get a Financial Life: Personal Finance in Your Twenties and Thirties*. New York: Simon and Schuster, Inc., 2009. Print.

Koski Research. "Charles Schwab 2011 Teens and Money Survey.", *About Schwab*. Charles Schwab. n.d. Web. 21 May 2012.

MacClanathan."4 Unhealthy Attitudes Toward Money." *Today*. MSNBC n.d. Web. 5 June 2012.

Mecham, Jesse. *You Need a Budget*, 2010, eBook.

Montague, David. *Essentials of Online Payment Security and Fraud Protection*. New York: John Wiley and Sons, Inc., 2011. Print.

Shellman, Jana. *Contract: What Credit Card Companies Don't Want You to Know*. Indiana: Threadbare Publishing, 2011. Print.

"Tax Revenues Fall in OECD Countries." *Documents*. OECD. 15 Dec. 2010. Web. 7 June 2012.

"What You Need to Know: New Credit Card Rules." *Consumer Info*. Federal Reserve Board of Governors. n.d. Web. 29 May 2012.

"What's in Your Score?" *Credit Education*. My FICO. n.d. Web. 5 June 2012.

About the Authors

Wes Karchut has over twenty five years of experience in business and finance. In addition to holding numerous senior-level management positions, he was a principal in a private equity technology fund. He received his M.B.A. in finance from the University of Wisconsin, Madison.

Darby Karchut has taught social studies at a nationally recognized junior high school for over fifteen years. She has received numerous educational awards — most recently a commendation from her school district for her contribution to teen literacy. She earned her M.Ed. from The Colorado College.

Further Reading

Bissonnette, Zac. *Debt Free U: How I paid for an Outstanding College Education without Loans, Scholarships or Mooching Off my Parents.* New York: Penguin Group, 2010. Print.

Orman, Suze. *The Money Book for the Young, Fabulous and Broke.* New York: RiverheadBooks, 2007. Print.

O'Shaughnessy, Lynn. *The College Solution: A Guide to Everyone Looking for the Right School at the Right Price.* New Jersey: FT Press, 2012. Print.

Ramsey, Dave *The Total Money Makeover: A Proven Plan For Financial Fitness.* Tennessee: Nelson Books, 2009. Print.

Index

D

E

amortization, 149
borrower, 26
car, 46
collateral, 147
conventional, 147
default, 48, 156
installment credit, 46
principal, 142
revolving credit, 42
secured, 147
term, 46, 60
unsecured loans, 147

M

minimum payment, 44
money personalities, 63
hoarders, 69
misers, 69
saver index, 70
spender index, 71
money skills, 4
mortgage, 26, 47, 149
loan to value ratio, 47

N

national debt, 136
needs, 17
net worth. *See* balance sheet

O

online bill payment, 129
online purchases, 165
overdraft protection, 123

P

PayPal, 129
payroll tax, 138
FICA, 138

Printed in Great Britain
by Amazon.co.uk, Ltd.,
Marston Gate.